PSYCHIC PANCAKES & COMMUNION PIZZA

Smyth & Helwys Publishing, Inc.
6316 Peake Road
Macon, Georgia 31210-3960
1-800-747-3016
©2011 by Smyth & Helwys Publishing
All rights reserved.
Printed in the United States of America.

The paper used in this publication meets the minimum requirements of
American National Standard for Information Sciences—
Permanence of Paper for Printed Library Materials.
ANSI Z39.48–1984. (alk. paper)

Cover illustration by Greg Cravens

Library of Congress Cataloging-in-Publication Data

Montgomery, Bert.
Psychic pancakes and communion pizza :
more musings and mutterings from a misfit / By Bert Montgomery.
p. cm.
Includes bibliographical references.
ISBN 978-1-57312-578-9 (pbk. : alk. paper)
1. Popular culture—Religious aspects—Christianity.
I. Title.
BR115.C8M6475 2011
286'.1092—dc22
[B]
2011004713

Psychic Pancakes & Communion Pizza
More Musings and Mutterings of a Church Misfit

Bert Montgomery

For Jency

Also by Bert Montgomery

This and other titles available from www. helwys.com

Contents

Foreword

When I got an e-mail from Bert Montgomery a couple of years ago telling me how much he enjoyed the book I had written about Duane Allman, I e-mailed him back a quick "thank you," just as I have to all the others who've sent me nice e-mails about *Skydog*.

The difference between Bert and virtually everyone else who e-mailed me about the book is that Bert *kept* e-mailing me. I was a tad leery at first, but when I found out he was a fellow author, I decided he must be an okay guy.

As it turns out, he's more than okay. I admire Bert because he writes about spiritual matters in worldly terms. If that seems like a contradiction, you might want to pull out your New Testament and read the parts in red ink. Just a suggestion.

Bert and I have never met each other in person. We've never spoken to each other on the phone. But I know Bert well, and we're Brothers with a capital "B." He grew up in the South. I grew up in the South. He's a writer. I'm a writer. He's a minister . . . . Well, two out of three is probably the best we could've hoped for.

On the following pages you'll get to know Bert Montgomery, too. He's funny, he's thoughtful, and he's thought provoking. Like I said, he writes of spiritual matters, but he manages to do so without making you feel like you've been thumped on the head with one of those hardcover Gideon hotel room Bibles.

On the title page of this book, Bert refers to himself as a "misfit." That's one more thing we have in common. Bert and I are both misfits, and we're both drawn to misfits—particularly the One with all that red ink in the New Testament.

—Randy Poe
Author, *Skydog: The Duane Allman Story*

Introduction

My first book, *Elvis, Willie, Jesus & Me: The Musings and Mutterings of a Church Misfit*, was a collection of articles I had written for an online community called Caleb's Cafe. Don't look for Caleb's Cafe; it doesn't exist anymore (which makes me sad). A few pieces had appeared in other places (newspapers, my private journal, or seminary writing assignments).

Likewise, the follow-up volume of musings and mutterings that is currently the object of your focused attention is a collection of articles I have written for an online community and pieces that have appeared in newspapers or on other web sites. The primary source is the Faith Lab (www.thefaithlab.com), which at the time of this publication is still very much alive and well (which makes me happy).

Some have also appeared in or at *The Commercial Dispatch*, MSDigitalDaily.com, EthicsDaily.com, and *Baptists Today*. My thanks to the editors of each of these entities for printing my ramblings.

To my editors and friends at Smyth & Helwys, thanks for being willing to do this a second time; to my church family at University Baptist, thanks for not just putting up with me, but also encouraging and supporting me and holding me accountable; and to David and David (they know who they are), thanks for direction, guidance, and patience. Thanks, thanks, and more thanks to artist extraordinaire Greg Cravens (www.cravenscartoon.com) for yet another fine cover illustration!

Part 1

Odds & Ends, Family & Friends

a collection of some seemingly unrelated musings
which did not fit in the other two sections,
but fit perfectly here
because they are about this and that,
and also about family and friends

Shall We Gather at the Tavern?

Once a month I gather with some friends where "good Baptists" ought not go . . . .

A funny thing happened during church last night: we were invited to participate in karaoke with the promise that everyone who sings gets a free shot of whatever liquor they want. No kidding.

Church + karaoke = a free shot of booze.

Actually it was quite exciting; usually everything at church goes according to plan, and everybody knows how to behave, act, and talk. Let's face it, "going to church" has become routine, common, and—dare I say it—*safe.*

But last night was different. First of all, it was on a Tuesday evening, not a Sunday morning or even a Wednesday night. Second, there was no planned music, no offering, not even a sermon. And finally, the majority of people present had no clue "church" was even happening.

Last night, "church" happened at Dave's Dark Horse Tavern in Starkville, Mississippi. Three men sat at a corner booth in a dimly lit pub. We were serenaded by classic rock, and we observed Holy Communion with Chicago-style deep (and I mean *deep*) dish pepperoni pizza and drinks.

Blasphemy? Maybe, but since Jesus was an accused blasphemer, I'm okay with that. Some friends and I have been gathering one night a month at the Tavern for discussions deeper than the deep dish pizza, and last night came the epiphany—we're having church. If church is the Body of Christ, if we believe Jesus that "wherever two or more are gathered in my name," then . . .

When we came together last night to share a meal and personal stories, and we gave thanks to God for "family" in whom we find God's strength, comfort, healing, and community, and we filled our time with laughter, reverence, irreverence, celebration, and, yes, prayer, then . . . we were in church.

There was something both humble and holy about meeting not in a specially designed place where everybody knows what's going on, but in a regular old bar, filled with all sorts of folks laughing, crying, playing pool, and consuming a variety of beverages. Something liberated us from playing the roles of "Christian" so that we could be real people expressing our hurts, doubts, hopes, and dreams. We were just plain folks enjoying the food and conversation.

And yet, there in the corner booth, a different kind of worship occurred—a genuine depth of holy fellowship in the presence of our Lord that I think is often absent in our planned-out, predictable, and set-apart services.

Don't get me wrong; there are many times when I need to "attend church" in the formal sense; there are many times when I need something reliable, comforting, and familiar because the world around me seems so strange and frightening. I'm not dismissing that. I'm just saying that "church" is *more* than that. It's *way* more than that.

Sometimes "church" happens in places we'd never imagine—even in a place of cursing, billiards, beer, and whiskey. And sometimes, even for Baptists like me, the Lord's Supper is not a tiny, prepackaged cracker and a shot of grape juice, but deep dish pizza and a refreshing beverage. Last night, the Body of Christ was becoming One.

So the next time you go out somewhere to eat with good friends, whether it's in a restaurant or even a tavern, maybe you'll have "church," too, and may God bless you for it. (Just remember that Jesus would tip twenty percent!)

Psychic Pancakes

(Ode to Ms. Sandy)

This is a story about Ms. Sandy Chilton.

Ms. Sandy was Poncho and Peadoo's mom. Poncho played first trumpet in the Destrehan High School band (that's in Destrehan, Louisiana); Peadoo played drums. I got to know Poncho and Peadoo when I transferred to Destrehan High School to start my sophomore year. Poncho graduated that year, joined the Navy, and got into the Navy Band, from which he just retired these twenty-plus years later.

Peadoo and I were both sophomores and went through the rest of high school together. We were the best of friends.

Occasionally, when I was hanging out with Peadoo at his house, Ms. Sandy would make us pancakes. Ms. Sandy made the absolute *best* pancakes I've ever had.

I left Destrehan in 1986, just a few weeks after high school graduation, and I've never lived in Louisiana again. Peadoo and I have kept up—not frequently, but we have always stayed in contact.

One day back in August I was making pancakes for my son and me, and as I flipped a cake, my mind wandered back to those days twenty-plus years ago when Peadoo and I would sit at the table and wait for Ms. Sandy to bring us fresh, hot pancakes. I've made pancakes a thousand times as a parent, and rarely if ever do I recall actually *thinking* about Ms. Sandy making pancakes while *I* was making pancakes, but this time I did.

A little later that same day, Peadoo called to tell me his mother was dying. It was a matter of time, maybe a day or two. And sure enough, the call about her death came a day or two later.

So am I psychic? Skilled in a little ESP? I don't think so.

I believe in the movement of the Holy Spirit. I believe God moves in mysterious ways. And I believe Ms. Sandy crossed my mind that day because she's dear to me, and I needed to pray for her and for her family—my friends.

Since Ms. Sandy's death, every time I make pancakes I think of her and of Peadoo and me sitting at the table, and I say a prayer. I say a prayer of thanksgiving for Ms. Sandy's life and the joy she shared with so many, and a prayer of thanks and a prayer of peace for my old friends, Peadoo and Poncho, and their families.

Riding Out the Storm

(Katrina, with Popcorn)

Back in August 2005, I was at home with my wife and sons, sleeping in my bed, and going on with the routines of my life in Kentucky. At the same time, Hurricane Katrina was destroying the Gulf Coast, levees were breaking, and water was inundating the city of my birth. My best friends from high school down in St. Charles Parish were forced to scatter; I learned later that some were in Florida, many had gone to Texas, and others into the Midwest.

Back in August 2005, while my life was going on as normal and while many of my friends were living in exile, Laura Grider Hansen was riding out the storm—and the ensuing chaos—on the fifth floor of East Jefferson General Hospital in Metairie.

Popcorn (I had always called Laura "Popcorn" because she went to our prom with my best friend, nicknamed "Peanut") is a nurse and had been for ten years when Katrina's winds began to blow. Her husband and children packed and left for Houston; Popcorn packed and left to spend an expected two days—at the *most*—working and living at the hospital.

The hurricane passed over with no direct hit on the New Orleans area. Still, trees were down, roofs were damaged, and hotels and offices had windows blown out. For many people in Louisiana, this was to be expected. "No big deal," Popcorn thought. "All fixable."

Of course, the electricity was out. A battery-powered radio served as the voice of the outside world to those inside East Jefferson Hospital, and the reports weren't good. Levees were failing. Water flowed through streets, overflowed the canals around the hospital, and soon reached the tops of houses.

The hospital's backup power kept the most necessary equipment working (like vents, pumps, etc.). Popcorn and her colleagues cared for patients using flashlights and wore headbands with lights. Air conditioning—even in August—was deemed a "nonessential luxury" and was lost halfway through the first full day.

Twelve-hour shifts for twelve straight days. Six nurses sharing an empty room. Sleeping on air mattresses.

"The radio and news broadcasts that everyone outside of New Orleans was seeing were very true: New Orleans was a war zone," Popcorn told me. "Although we didn't have a lot of trouble at East Jefferson, we were still kept under lock and key and only allowed to move about in the parking garage." The National Guard made hourly rounds on the unit to make sure everything was okay. Popcorn said the Guard members were "a pleasure to have around; they made you feel safe and secure when everything else around us was not."

Popcorn and her colleagues befriended a couple of Guardsmen, and those men took the nurses out through the streets near City Park. Riding in military vehicles, Popcorn helped deliver water, food, diapers, baby formula, ice, and personal hygiene supplies to anyone who needed them.

Twelve—not two, but *twelve*—days later, she was able to go home and rest. While her husband and children were still in Houston, Popcorn went to her parents' house in LaPlace. They had just returned home a couple of days earlier. "I was so exhausted and mentally drained," Popcorn said. "I passed out on their sofa until noon the next day."

As for Popcorn's own damages, there were trees down—even one that fell onto her son's upstairs bedroom; some roof and other property damage, but nothing that couldn't be repaired. After two weeks, her family returned home, only to have to evacuate again a couple of weeks later. "Yep," she said, "I was back in gear heading to the hospital for Hurricane Rita."

Popcorn is reflective: "If it had not been for the wonderful group of staff members I worked with, it would have been very different. We laughed and cried together, sometimes at the same time. We all had our moments of weakness; I truly missed my family, my dog, my own bed."

Laura was a cute little freshman band member when we met during my senior year. Twenty-plus years later and still stuck with the nickname "Popcorn" (at least as far as I'm concerned), she's now a hero who inspires me.

Thanks be to God for Popcorn, and all the others who, like her, willingly devote their lives to truly caring for others.

Of Pirates and Swine

Not to disparage the seriousness of the swine flu, nor the need for public safety regarding it, but this was written during the first round of swine-flu hysteria.

I've started keeping a short list of reasons why Facebook is the greatest thing since chicory coffee. Here is reason number one: pirates and swine.

Yesterday was a *long* day filled with highs and lows. I came home and there on my Facebook were notes aplenty posted from everybody about the swine flu: from "precautions-to-take" and "schools-in-Texas-closing" postings to "doomsday-paranoia" or "shut-up-and-relax-and-just-live-your-life" comments. As word has leaked out that I have had some theological education, a few Christian friends asked my thoughts on the swine flu and the predicted pandemic, particularly in light of the question, "Are we living in the last days?"

My first reaction was that if anybody is trusting *me* to carry God's timetable, we're all in trouble. But I carefully worded this reply to the first friend who asked, then began to share it with a few others as the opportunities arose:

> Well, to be totally honest, I remember reading that Jesus said he doesn't even know the day or the hour, so just leave that up to God and do the things Jesus tells us to do: care for the sick and widows and orphans, help the poor, love your enemies, and love God and everyone else, too. If it turns into a worldwide epidemic, we care for the sick with love and patience, we help the poor, we love our enemies, and we pray and love God and each other.

And if it's the end of the world, Jesus will return and find us faithful. If it's not, a few hundred years from now people will look back at us like we look back at the bubonic plague in the 1300s and say "that was pretty bad, but look at those guys running around saying it's the end of the world!" . . .

After sending this response, I discovered that you can change the language of your Facebook to "English (Pirate)," and my life has been nothing but laughter since. And that's why I love Facebook. Because it makes it super easy to stay in touch with a lot of folks I have known in many different places over many years, and it allows us to ask each other important questions and stay updated on the swine flu. Then I can sit back and enjoy something as simple as pirate translations of "1 friend request" ("1 sorry lout thinks they're your matey") and "I like this" ("Arrrrr, this be pleasin' to me eye").

Facebook. Pirates and swine. I hope that Jesus doesn't find me paranoid and forgetting to do the things he tells us to do, but instead that he finds me faithful, and maybe even with a little piratey joy, too! Arrrrrr!

Who Dat?!

(The '09 Saints and a Requiem for a Joke)

This was written just after the Saints' thirteenth straight victory, and prior to an end-of-the-season three-game losing streak. Of course, we all know the Saints went on to beat the Colts in the Super Bowl. Just remember, this was originally published before *the playoffs.*

The New Orleans Saints have a perfect record and are serious contenders for the Super Bowl. That *used* to be the punch line of countless jokes; it was guaranteed to get a laugh every time. In high school, we'd laugh as we'd chant, "Who dat?! Who dat say dey gonna beat dem Saints? Who dat?!" Because, of course, just about *everybody* would beat dem Saints.

But the joke is no more. The New Orleans Saints have a perfect record so far this season—with three games left to go—and they are indeed serious contenders for the Super Bowl. Only one other team in the NFL remains undefeated—the Indianapolis Colts, led by Peyton Manning, the son of everybody's favorite Saint, Archie Manning.

A Manning versus the Saints in the Super Bowl. *It is possible.*

And it couldn't have come at a better time. Just over four years since Hurricane Katrina, the Gulf Coast region is still rebuilding and still healing. But now there's an expectant fervor in the air.

As a former resident of Louisiana (I was born in the Big Easy), I wept and mourned during Katrina and in the months that followed. Raised in St. Charles Parish (I'm a 1986 graduate of Destrehan High School—Go Cats!), I was filled with righteous indignation every time some ignorant preacher pronounced Katrina to be God's judgment upon New Orleans.

But today, rather than mourning, I am celebrating. Up here in Starkville, Mississippi, I'm dancing the Second Line. Up here at Mississippi State University, a bunch of us are doing the Benson Boogie.

Standing in the checkout line recently at the local grocery store, I spotted black and gold items amid all the maroon and white t-shirts, mugs, and license plates. Forget the swine flu. Saints fever has become an epidemic!

Naturally, I couldn't be more excited for my friends down in Louisiana. Heck, all hurricanes aside, Saints fans have suffered for more than forty years.

Some of the first words I learned to speak after "Momma" and "Daddy" were "poor Archie; poor, poor Archie."

It was the Saints who gave the lowly Tampa Bay Buccaneers their first ever franchise win after twenty-six straight losses, prompting a radio parody of Randy Newman's 1977 hit "Short People," targeting Saints head coach Hank Stram ("Short Coaches . . . they can't even beat Tampa Bay!").

And then came 1980. Instead of counting 4 and 0, 9 and 0, and 13 and 0 like this year (2009), fans wore bags over their heads and kept a different count: 0 and 4, 0 and 9, 0 and 13!

I was there when we dropped the "S" and the Saints became the "Aints." I remember people singing "Send in the Clowns" instead of "When the Saints Go Marching In." At least one church tried to turn the "Aints" into an opportunity for evangelism—the sign at a prominent suburban Baptist congregation once boasted that "Saints win HERE every Sunday!"

Now, though, I'm getting the sense from my friends in Louisiana that Mardi Gras has come several months early.

"The atmosphere here is *great*!" writes my friend Popcorn. "It has definitely lifted the spirits of everyone. After Katrina, the Saints were the only thing people looked forward to; it lifted the spirits to see that there was some sort of normalcy back in New Orleans. By the way, check out my Christmas tree this year—Black & Gold, Baby!"

Geesh (hard "G," rhymes with *leash*), another close friend, reports, "I see Saints fans expressing themselves everywhere. There are signs all over the place; . . . jerseys and t-shirts on anything with a pulse. There is a feeling that this is another in a long list of pretty positive things that shows that we are coming back from the storm."

Though she is not a big football fan, even Doonbie, my former high school band drum major, is excited about this great season: "I personally love it because when the Saints play, Walmart is empty and that is when I get my grocery shopping done in peace and solitude."

Four years ago, a few preachers were "celebrating" God's "judgment" on New Orleans. I wouldn't be surprised if some preacher today has found a way to connect the book of Revelation to the New Orleans Saints as proof that the end is near.

All I know is that even though I've been away from the Crescent City for more than twenty years, the depths of my despair resulting from Katrina have finally been matched by the heights of my pride in the New Orleans Saints. And all I know is that, as of this writing, the NFL team formerly known as the "Aints" have a perfect 13 wins and 0 losses. And in Louisiana, that is spelled "thirteen and eaux."

Who dat?! Who dat, indeed! We're all smiling, but ain't *nobody* laughing anymore.

Ferris Bueller and the
Houston Valet

Recently I was in Houston, Texas, for the Cooperative Baptist Fellowship General Assembly. I drove from Starkville, Mississippi, to Houston in a nice, sporty, blue 2009 Toyota Camry with a CD player and stereo sound that couldn't be beat—rented from the nice folks at Budget.

Two-star hotels on the edge of town usually get my business, but for conventions—with budgeted money to cover the cost of my attending such things—I pulled into one of those fancy convention center hotels where they have sharply dressed people who will do everything for you.

Arriving at the downtown Houston hotel reserved for CBF guests, I realized, like Dorothy stepping out into the land of Oz, that I wasn't at your neighborhood Super 8 anymore. For one thing, the folks at my usual lodging locations have *never* met me at my car to open the door for me, greet me, unload my luggage, or offer to park my car.

I handed the car key to the sharply dressed and polite young man outside the hotel lobby. When I inquired about a place to eat nearby, I learned that the fancy downtown Houston hotel offers a complimentary downtown shuttle because it doesn't share a parking lot with Waffle Houses, Pizza Huts, or Burger Kings like the Motel 6s I am accustomed to.

Freddie, a former Houston Cougars football player, drove a sharp, black Lincoln Navigator to the front of the hotel, picked up my sons and me, and drove us to a fancy pizza establishment a few blocks away (this wasn't your average pizza joint). He left us with a number to call when we finished. We enjoyed our pizza from the fine establishment, called the hotel number Freddie gave us, and then, as promised, Freddie arrived in the sharp, black Lincoln Navigator and drove us back to our fancy downtown Houston hotel.

Once we returned, we asked the sharply dressed, polite young man holding the door open for us if we could go into the garage to retrieve our camera from the rental car. "Oh no!" he said. They would bring the car to us, let us retrieve our camera, and then they would park it again at no cost to us and no trouble to them.

Then he noticed my name. Uh-oh.

"Mr. Montgomery, you're going to have to come with me." This is *not* what you want to hear from a sharply dressed hotel clerk.

"There's been a minor incident with your vehicle," the valet said calmly as we followed him to the parking garage. "It's a rental car, is that correct?"

"Um, yes. What *kind* of incident?"

It seemed the valet driving our Camry pulled out in front of an oncoming truck. Fortunately, nobody was hurt; in fact, the truck suffered no damage at all. As for the Camry's front end, one thing was for sure—the nice, sporty, blue 2009 Toyota Camry with the CD player and stereo sound that couldn't be beat, rented from the nice folks at Budget, would *not* be the vehicle that carried us back to Starkville.

The manager began talking about forms, signatures, about their taking *full* responsibility with insurance companies and Budget, but all I could hear and see was that infamous scene from *Ferris Bueller's Day Off* in which the parking attendant says, "Trust me, I'm a professional," then takes Ferris's friend's father's red 1961 Ferrari out for a joy ride.

Okay, so a sporty blue 2009 Toyota Camry is a far cry from a two-door red-hot sports car. It was a sweet ride nonetheless, and the thought of a valet tearing through the streets of downtown Houston in our rented sedan was more than I could bear.

This was funny. *Seriously* funny.

In all fairness to the valet and the parking management company, I did learn that the accident occurred inside the garage, not on the streets of Houston. The valet had attempted to straighten the Camry in a parking space, and a truck coming down the aisle had hit it.

But in all fairness to me, I did begin laughing at the Ferris Bueller image racing through my mind, and I continued laughing even after they explained the boring manner in which the incident actually happened.

As best I can tell, there are at least two important lessons we can learn from this: (1) when going to Cooperative Baptist Fellowship General Assemblies, it is best to rent a car rather than drive your own, because you never know what those fancy hotel people do once they have your car keys; and (2) whatever you do, do *not* ever buy a used, sporty, blue 2009 Toyota Camry from anyone, regardless of the promises made about its history.

Makin' a Joyful Noise!

(God and the Derek Trucks Band)

When I was in high school, I loved going to an Assembly of God church with my friends from time to time. To be honest, it was not so much for the preaching as for the music; they knew that lively, improvisational music speaks the unspeakable words of the Spirit. At those charismatic worship services, we all let the music guide the movement of our bodies in worship with the Spirit.

I remember looking around and noticing that even though some people stood still, their eyes were closed with their faces lifted toward heaven, and their heads were nodding gently, peacefully, as though the music were praying and praising for them. All around me, others clapped and danced; many lifted their hands high above their heads as though reaching toward the Eternal, or as though surrendering completely to the Spirit that was moving.

"Worshiping *in* the Spirit" is how many referred to it. I guess that's why I always loved visiting charismatic worship services—the music was *alive* and *celebratory*, and I heard God, I sensed God, I was dancing in the *presence* of God in a deeply transcendent mystery beyond mere words.

One Tuesday evening not long ago, I closed my eyes, soaking in the sounds and answering the repeated charge to "make a joyful noise," and I worshiped *in* the Spirit of God.

Make a joyful noise! Nothing's more biblical than that (it is an oft-repeated instruction in Psalms, after all). People around me that Tuesday night let the music move their bodies; some stood with their eyes closed and heads lifted, nodding gently and peacefully. Others clapped and danced; many lifted their hands high above their heads.

But far from being in a charismatic church's worship service, I was in an Oxford, Mississippi, club surrounded by a jubilant crowd at a Derek Trucks Band concert.

I guess that's why I have always loved live concerts—the music is *alive* and *celebratory*, and I hear God, I sense God, I dance in the *presence* of God in a deeply transcendent mystery beyond mere words.

Some will quickly point out that there is a huge difference between a charismatic church service and a live concert at a club; and, in many ways, they may be right. But I've always been able to sense a transcendent, mysterious spirit moving in the depths of my soul whenever I am experiencing (not just listening, but *experiencing*) great, lively, improvisational music. For me—I can't speak for anybody else—just as I worshiped *in* the Spirit as great bands played celebratory praise music at the Assembly of God church, I also worshiped *in* the Spirit as the Derek Trucks Band invited us all to make a joyful noise.

Some people I know are not churchgoers; some people I know do not call themselves Christians; some people I know claim no religious belief at all. However, when we start talking about music, we always end up speechless when trying to describe this mysterious experience we share.

I've decided that, as sure as people who would never describe themselves as "Christian" or even "religious" can be awestruck and speechless in the depths of their beings when standing in the mysterious presence of the wonders of nature—which I believe to be God's voice calling out to us—then people can be awestruck and speechless in the mysterious presence that moves and "speaks" through music—which I also believe to be God's voice calling out to us.

That same Tuesday evening, I had the opportunity to sit down with Kofi Burbridge, who plays keyboards, organ, and flute with the Derek Trucks Band. We talked about his musical influences, his family, and "spirituality" as he senses it through music. Kofi claims no particular religious faith or tradition, but he is quick to acknowledge something mysteriously transcendent going on in music that gets to the depths, the core, of one's existence.

I understand and appreciate what Kofi is talking about. I choose to wrap the words of my faith around it and believe that God is calling out to us and communicating His love to our souls. If someone consciously chooses *not* to wrap such religious terminology around it, that doesn't discount that they are experiencing something real nonetheless.

We can embrace the mystery through music. With songs like "Joyful Noise," "Soul Serenade," and "Already Free," the Derek Trucks Band *gets* it.

CDs and Pen Pals

(*Owed* to Heather McCready)

This piece tells about how I first heard of Heather McCready. She has since released another CD and is working on a third. Check her out at www.heathermccready.com.

Some time ago, I started keeping a list of reasons I like Facebook (see "Of Pirates and Swine"). For a while, I ran out of reasons to write of my affection for Facebook . . . until now. Without further ado, here are more reasons why I love Facebook: making new friends, discovering new music, and sharing faith stories.

More specifically, all rolled into one, I love it because of Heather McCready.

Sure, it's scary the way friends of friends of friends of some relative's friends ask to be your friend, and if I'm not worried about some weirdo I don't know wanting to befriend me, I'm worried that somebody is thinking "who is this weirdo?" when I send out the occasional friend request.

But sometimes, like the long-gone golden age of "pen pals" that I've heard so much about, Facebook connects people who become friends because of written communication about life. And death. And music. And faith.

Which brings me back to Heather. A guy I've never met somehow stumbled upon the Facebook group page for my first book, and then he and I eventually became "approved" Facebook friends (he has excellent taste in music, by the way). Later, he sent one of those "friend suggestions" to me, suggesting that Heather and I be friends.

Okay.

Little did I know he was "introducing" me to a wonderful singer/songwriter. Next thing I know, I'm listening to her songs, she's reading my musings, and we're "talking" about the dark struggles of faith that some folks just have to live with. And I can't stop listening to her songs.

Her CD is called *Finally Free,* and the only way I can describe it is by taking the best of Iris Dement, the best of Allison Krauss, the best of Emmylou Harris, the best of *Windsong*-era John Denver, adding a pinch of Simon and Garfunkel and just a hint of Joni Mitchell, and coming up with something close to Heather's music.

There are songs about love and faithfulness and marriage. Songs about children. Songs about pain. Songs about searching. Songs about Jesus.

And then there's "Scarborough Fair." It's not a cover of the Simon and Garfunkel classic, but a hauntingly mystically beautiful homage to the Simon and Garfunkel classic. You'll just have to listen to it for yourself. Go visit her webpage, read about her, listen to the songs she's posted, and then follow the links on her page to purchase the CD. Trust me.

For the last few days, I have been wild about Facebook again because of new friends, faith stories, connecting my new friend with other friends, and because I have a new favorite CD that I just can't turn off.

You're Bloody Well Right!

(Of Bela Lugosi and Deeper Chalices)

I gave blood a couple of days ago. No, I didn't play rugby. I reclined in one of those blood-drive tour buses, let a nice nurse stick a needle in my left arm, and thought about stuff while she filled a little plastic bag with my blood.

Naturally, I thought about some of my favorite blood-related songs: U2's "Sunday Bloody Sunday"; Dylan's "It's Alright, Ma (I'm Only Bleeding)"; and, of course, Supertramp's "Bloody Well Right" (if you've got to get a song stuck in your head for a day, it might as well be a good one).

I thought about some of my favorite blood-related movies, and I could hear Bela Lugosi's thick Hungarian pronunciation of "blood" as he portrayed Count Dracula; I could hear Tony Perkins as Norman Bates exclaiming, "Mother . . . Mother! Blood! Blood!"; and I could hear Charlton Heston as Moses declaring, "Soylent Green is people!" (which didn't make any sense; maybe I have my Heston movies mixed up).

I thought about an early *M*A*S*H* episode I had recently watched—a wounded white soldier made sure the doctors and nurses knew not to give him any of that "darkie" blood. His racist remarks opened the door for a great lesson from master teachers Hawkeye and Trapper.

I thought of my mother—she'd probably want to see a legal document, signed and stamped by a notary public, that the blood she was about to receive did not come from anybody remotely connected, in any possible way, to the LSU Tigers.

Then I thought about some of *my* blood flowing through *another's* veins—and that maybe, just maybe, regardless of class, age, ethnicity, religion, gender, or politics, that person may eventually develop a new-found fondness for the Ramones, *Attack of the Killer Tomatoes*, Dolly Parton, Eldridge Cleaver, and Pee-Wee Herman.

And I thought about Jesus' blood.

Morbid, huh?

But blood is at the core of two thousand years' worth of Christian doctrine. Blood was shed; blood gives life. "What can wash away my sins?" asks the favorite old hymn.

"This is my blood, drink it and remember me," Jesus says, sharing wine with the disciples. Variations of this saying are heard all around the world in Christian services (sometimes weekly, monthly, or once a quarter if you're a Baptist) as people sip from a cup, dip bread or a wafer into a chalice, or gulp down the tiniest possible amount of grape juice from a tiny plastic shot glass.

Essentially, we are telling ourselves we are drinking blood (you can insert your own Bela Lugosi joke here, if you are so inclined). And while we laugh at the ignorance of that white soldier on *M*A*S*H* who was afraid of being contaminated by "colored" blood; and while I laugh at my mother when I think of her ever receiving "LSU" blood; and while we all laugh at a world transformed into peace-loving country-punk lovers of justice and good comedy when everyone gets some of my blood, here's hoping and praying that regular consumption of Jesus' blood may actually "contaminate" our own.

Here's hoping and praying that regular consumption of Jesus' blood may begin to transform us into people of service, patience, humility, goodness, self-control, forgiveness, and, above all, love, sweet love. Love, *bloody* love.

Evidence suggests it hasn't worked too well so far.

Maybe we need more wine (fellow Baptists, read "grape juice") and bigger, deeper chalices (fellow Baptists, read "bigger, deeper plastic shot glasses"), and to drink it weekly, if not daily (fellow Baptists, read "dump the once-a-quarter nonsense and drink up!").

Now, if you'll excuse me, I'm going to research famous lines from *The Ten Commandments*.

Family, Friends, and Race

(Ode to Race, part 1)

This was written on January 23, 2009, in light of the events surrounding the inauguration of the first African American as president of the United States. I had been reflecting on my own forty years of life in the post-civil rights era South. This is the first of three musings on race and faith.

I can't recall hearing my parents say the word "nigger," unless it was in the context of a quote, and even then, they never seemed comfortable saying it.

Dad was born and raised in the southwest Mississippi woods—between Brookhaven and McComb. He can remember the first time he ever saw a person with dark skin. I asked him to tell me the story again (the older we both get, the more I ask my parents to retell their stories).

"Dad, tell me again—how old were you and where were you when you recall seeing a black person for the first time?"

"I don't recall exactly, but I must have been about six years old. I was playing in the sandbed by the side of the road, down the hill from Mamma and Pa's house. Looking up, I saw this large colored woman (as they were then known) walking down the hill toward me. I do recall being quite scared, because she was between me and the house. Her name was Louella Cook, and she had been doing housework that day for a neighbor and was walking along the wagon trails through the woods back to her house which was a couple of miles farther on from Pa's house. Ever after, when Louella saw my Mama, she would laugh and tell how she had scared 'that white chile' when he saw her coming toward him down the hill! Of course, you must remember, we didn't see many people of any color in the early 1940s, way out there in the woods where we lived, so any stranger would have frightened me."

As for me, in Louisiana, just outside of New Orleans during the 1970s and 1980s (I was born in the Big Easy in 1968), I was always interacting with African Americans. We went to school together, played on the playground together, and played in the school bands together. At home, my family and I watched television shows like *The Jeffersons* and *What's Happening*, in which black folks and white folks were figuring out how to live together in a new integrated society.

And yet I never thought a black man would be president, at least not in my lifetime.

Not too long ago, Dad gave me his hardback first edition copy of *To Kill a Mockingbird* (a book of which he always spoke fondly). So, in honor of Dr. Martin Luther King Jr.'s birthday this past Monday, and on the eve of a historic inauguration, I gathered my wife and sons around the television to watch the brilliant film adaptation of the Harper Lee masterpiece.

I wanted Rob and Daniel to have some grasp of the transformation in the South—in my parents' lifetime and even to some degree in mine—from "niggers" and "nigger-lovers" to black folks and white folks not only going to school together and eating in restaurants together, but finally beginning to share power together for the good of all. We have a long way to go, that's for sure, but we've come a long, long way since Dad's first encounter with a person of a different color some sixty-plus years ago.

For that, I give thanks to God!

A Mississippi Delta Girl

(Ode to Race, part 2)

The experiences of my parents, who were born and raised in post-Depression pre-civil rights Mississippi, are far different from my own; I was born and raised in the post-civil rights middle-class suburbs outside New Orleans. Before I can share some of my experiences, I need to share my parents' stories. This second story is one my mother shared of being raised in Tunica County. These are her words.

While Bob [my husband] and I are both Mississippians, raised in loving families (parents, siblings, grandparents, aunts, uncles, and cousins) with the same values and deeply held religious beliefs, our cultural backgrounds are vastly different.

Growing up in a rural community in the southwestern part of the state, Bob can remember the first time he saw a "colored" person. I cannot. Having been born in the Delta, I found that "colored people" were always a part of my life.

In 1944 (I was four), Daddy bought a fairly good-sized farm. On this farm there were several colored families who were known to the other farmers in the area as "Henry's Negroes" (pronounced NIG-rah in the South). This was to distinguish them from "Mr. Boyd's Negroes" or "Peck's Negroes." Most of these families lived and worked on the same farm for years. They were paid a salary, provided housing with a plot of land to raise a garden, and given medical care and whatever other needs might arise.

I especially remember Charlotte and Will, whose house was only a few feet from ours. While Will was older and unable to do much work, he was always around and could be depended upon to entertain a child with a good story or a game of checkers. Charlotte occasionally helped Mama, mostly with ironing and heavy house cleaning in the spring before revival when the preachers had to be fed. When Mama and Daddy would go to town (Tunica), Charlotte and Will would stay with my sister, my brother, and me.

Charlotte and Will moved away around the time I was in junior high. Years later, after Will died, Charlotte moved back. By this time I was away at college. After graduate school, while I was home getting ready for my wedding, my sister and I took Charlotte to Memphis several times for cancer treatments and finally admitted her to the hospital where she died shortly after I was married.

I will never forget Will and Charlotte, who helped raise me.

A Stream of (Honky) Consciousness

(Ode to Race, part 3)

The first two installments of this series involved sharing experiences of my mother and father who were born and raised in pre-civil rights era Mississippi. This is a broad, personal observation, coming from a white man born and raised in the aftermath of the 1960s civil rights era in the South. This was written on February 5, 2009.

I was born in New Orleans on Thursday, March 14, 1968. That's exactly three weeks prior to the day Dr. Martin Luther King, Jr., was assassinated in Memphis (another large southern city I call home).

I grew up laughing at Richard Pryor on the television (where he was censored and "safe"). His guest appearance with a young Lou Gossett, Jr. (with hair!), on an early *Partridge Family* episode ranks as one of my favorite shows of all time.

I remember staying up late and watching Pryor on *Saturday Night Live*. At school, we (white and black kids) would all go around imitating him as the priest on the SNL spoof of *The Exorcist*. But the appearance I remembered most is from the classic (and initially controversial) *Saturday Night Live* "Word Association" sketch in which Pryor and Chevy Chase trade racial slurs. When I got into high school and finally saw *Blazing Saddles* (thanks to the advent of VHS rentals), it made perfect sense that Richard Pryor was one of the writers of this brilliant satire of racism.

I also remember his transformation. It seemed newsworthy in 1979 that when Richard Pryor returned from visiting Africa, he vowed never to use the word "nigger" again.

This past weekend, I attended the New Baptist Covenant Southeast Regional meeting. I stood, sat, walked around, and worshiped inside the 16th Street Baptist Church in Birmingham, Alabama—the very same church building that was bombed with dynamite on a Sunday morning in 1963, killing four young African-American girls and injuring more than twenty others who had gathered to learn about Jesus.

I walked around this building along with many others, sensing we were treading on sacred ground. I sat in worship with whites and blacks sitting together, praying together, and celebrating God together. I sat in total silence when Kate Campbell got up to sing her song "Bear It Away"—a song about the 1963 bombing.

Kate stood at the podium, guitar in hand, to sing that song, and . . . well, I can't fathom what she must have felt as she looked out over the sanctuary now filled with blacks and whites together; as she looked out to the corner of the church where the dynamite exploded; as she looked up and saw the stained glass picture of Jesus that had been repaired after the bombing blew off his face. For a moment there was a lump in everyone's throats, including Kate's.

Like Richard Pryor, maybe our nation has finally made a transformation. For the late comedian, it meant abandoning a word that helped make him famous, a word that for him ceased to be funny in light of its degrading and hate-filled usage.

For us, who knows? But there was something redemptive, transformational, and holy going on that weekend inside the 16th Avenue Baptist Church, and all politics aside, there *is* something redemptive, transformational, and, yes, holy, going on when our nation elects an African-American man to be president.

I-Feel-Like-I'm-Fixin'-To . . .

(A Peacenik Reflects on Veterans' Day)

Written on Veterans' Day 2009.

Uncle Obed, from over in the northern Mississippi Delta, drove a mobile medic truck during World War II. His son, my cousin Ricky, says the stories Uncle Obed told resembled the chaos that was made famous by *M*A*S*H* (even though that was set in Korea). Uncle Obed returned from Europe and continued farming in the Delta.

Cousin Roffie, from down in Brookhaven, Mississippi, built bridges in Vietnam with the Army Corps of Engineers. He returned and taught civil engineering at Mississippi State until his retirement a few years ago.

John, a good friend up in northern Kentucky, served in the first Gulf War. Today he's back in his hometown—married with kids and a full-time job, and a leader in his church.

Me? I've always been more of the conscientious objector type because of my strong religious views. It's Christian pacifism mixed with being born in 1968.

I grew up idolizing the hippies of the 1960s. Since childhood, I've known every word to Country Joe McDonald's "I-Feel-Like-I'm-Fixin'-to-Die Rag" (the Woodstock version), and I still consider Edwin Starr's "War" as one of my all-time favorite songs.

Favorite presidential candidate? Gene McCarthy.

Favorite Broadway musical? *Hair.*

Favorite Beatle? John, of course (with George and Ringo tied at a close second).

So when my high school friends were going to Kuwait for Operation Desert Storm, I had already grown shoulder-length hair, become an Abbie Hoffman pseudo-scholar, and was on my way to Washington, D.C., for a protest march with other students and friends of the Southern Baptist Theological Seminary.

In my early twenties, life was clearly black and white for me. I was right and my friends (and everyone else) in the military were wrong. I had studied philosophical and Christian ethics, learned the truth, and arrived at the mature and correct conclusions.

But as Bob Dylan has said, "I was so much older then; I'm younger than that now."

Then came Somalia. Darfur. September 11, 2001.

My easy, peacenik answers are too simple for me now.

Not only that, but I recently learned that my cousin Billy was in the National Guard and called up to Ole Miss to keep the peace when the federal government said James Meredith could study there. I can't imagine what that must have been like.

Over the past several years, I became friends with Phil, a Korean War veteran who shared his personal struggles with returning to rural Kentucky farming life after being in combat.

And in my mid-30s, I grew to love David, a Vietnam War veteran who, after tours of duty there, returned home and remained active in the National Guard until just a few years ago, when he entered his sixties.

Billy has a heart of gold and will go out of his way to help anybody. Phil is a quiet, gentle soul, who—though a church deacon—is very much at home with and able to love some really tough folks who have lived rough lives. And David is the kindest, most welcoming, most loving, and most unselfish man I think I may have ever met.

I have fond memories of Uncle Obed from my childhood, and I am quite proud of his service during the Second World War.

Cousin Roffie and I attended some MSU baseball games together when I was a student there. I once asked him to tell me stories about being in Vietnam; he declined. I've met some of his former civil engineering students, and they tell me that though he was a tough instructor, they are far better engineers because of him.

I'd trust my friend John with my life. I learned from talking with him that war really is hell. John responded to his call to serve our nation and has every right to be proud of it—and I'm proud of him for it.

Yes, I still know (and honestly, still love) all the words to "I-Feel-Like-I'm-Fixin'-To-Die." Yes, I still consider myself a bit of a Christian pacifist.

But my "adult" certainty—my need to be right and my need to set my views over and against other people's—has eroded over the years. In its place is emerging a more childlike appreciation for mystery. In its place is growing a deeper appreciation of and respect for people who experience life differently than I do.

That is something I didn't used to have; I was indeed so much older then, but by the grace of God, I'm younger than that now.

Birthday Elvis
8 & 42

Just in case it isn't obvious, this was written on January 2010, and the Saints were entering the playoffs.

Number 8. January 8, to be exact. It's Elvis's birthday.

Number 8. Archie Manning wore the number 8 on his jersey. He is everyone's all-time favorite Saint. Speaking of the New Orleans Saints, at 13-3, they are undeniably one of the best teams in the NFL (so what if they lost these last three games?) and are going into the playoffs. I'm pulling for them to make it into the Super Bowl.

But Archie's not leading the Saints anymore. It's Drew Brees. I've got a Saints' fleur-de-lis sticker on my car that says "Brees'N thru the Season!" and has the number 9 with a halo around it—Mr. Brees wears the number 9.

Number 9. Number 9. Number 9.

The Number 9 is not the number 8, and it brings to mind John Lennon and the Beatles, which is not the topic of this essay. It's Elvis. But then again, Lennon and the Beatles *loved* Elvis . . . .

Birthday Elvis number 8.

And number 42.

Forty-two is, as everyone knows, the answer to the ultimate question of life, the universe, and everything. But the late Douglas Adams reminds us that while everyone knows the answer is 42, nobody knows what the ultimate question is.

Nevertheless, 42. Elvis was 42 when he died—assuming you're one of those people who believe he's dead.

My second-favorite Elvis-is-or-is-not-dead theory is purported by the Tommy Lee Jones character in *Men in Black*: "Elvis didn't die; he just went home." Like you, I've been tempted to believe that at times.

The more plausible explanation, and my personal favorite Elvis-is-or-is-not-dead theory, is presented in one of the greatest movies of the last decade, *Bubba Ho-Tep*. Elvis didn't die—he just switched places with an impersonator, and the impersonator died. The real Elvis lives in a nursing home in the middle-of-nowhere Texas and is friends with John F. Kennedy (whose skin was dyed black by the conspirators—which included LBJ—after he survived the assassination attempt, and he was left at the nursing home to be forever known as a crazy-old-black-man-who-thinks-he's-JFK). Together, Elvis and Jack fight an ancient Egyptian mummy that is wreaking havoc at the nursing home.

Back to 42. Elvis was 42 when the impersonator died and the whole world thought *he* died (or whatever you explanation you prefer).

I turn 42 in March. I feel like I'm just beginning to live. Kind of like Elvis getting his groove back in the nursing home and kicking a mummy's behind. At 42 (or on the edge of 42—but that conjures up Stevie Nicks memories, which are best saved for another story), I feel like I'm finally finding my groove in this life. I sense that I am not alone, which may be why some consider 42 to be the answer to the ultimate question of life, the universe, and everything.

Heck, at 42 (or the edge of 42), I'm witnessing the Saints have home field advantage in the playoffs for the first time ever, and possibly even hosting the NFC Championship.

Which goes back to number 9. Drew Brees. And before Drew, there was Archie.

Number 8. January 8. Elvis's birthday. Even before his "retirement" (however you wish to define "retirement"), Elvis has always been a defining point of reference for my life. I guess he'll always be—especially if I'm fighting off mummies as an old man in a nursing home.

Anyway, happy birthday, Elvis—wherever you are.

A Farewell to Farrah, but Not *Really*

(Ode to Memories and Mystery)

Composed in July 2009.

Farrah Fawcett, whose poster was on just about every boy's wall in the mid-1970s, and who much later starred in one of my favorite movies, *The Apostle*—GONE.

Pontchartrain Beach amusement park in New Orleans, which is where I won the poster of then Farrah Fawcett-Majors by throwing darts at balloons or something like that—GONE. It's also where my Bogue Chitto, Mississippi, cousins and my family would go when they all came down to visit us in Louisiana. Roller coasters, haunted houses, cousins and laughter, and Mammaw and Pappaw sitting on benches watching us wander all over the park. Pontchartrain Beach is most definitely a long time GONE.

Ed McMahon, whom my cousin Jeff and I used to stay up and watch on Carson's *Tonight Show* back when I was a little kid spending a week in Bogue Chitto with cousins and grandparents—GONE.

My grandparents' house in which cousin Jeff and I used to stay up late as kids and watch Carson and Ed McMahon—GONE. Not totally, but sort of. The family sold all the land and the house, and now strangers live there; everything is different and strange. Mammaw's and Pappaw's house is GONE.

My great-grandmother's house up on the hill above Mammaw's and Pappaw's house in Bogue Chitto—GONE. My cousins Jennifer and Jenene had a little record player in that house, and my sister, Becky, and I used to go with our cousins to play inside the old house (my dad was born in that old house) and listen to 45s, including cute little Michael Jackson singing "Rockin' Robin." Now we can't even get up the hill to see where the old house used to stand because the road has washed out—it's GONE.

Cute little Michael Jackson, whose "Rockin' Robin" has always brought back great childhood memories of cousins and Bogue Chitto, Mississippi—GONE.

The house in Destrehan, Louisiana, into which my family moved when I was ten years old (1978) and where my next door neighbor would come over to play basketball and sing songs from Michael Jackson's *Off the Wall* album—GONE. Again, not really: that house still stands, and it looks great (a former high school classmate now lives in it with her family, and I wish them all the enjoyment my family and I had there). But nevertheless, no Montgomerys have lived there in more than twenty-three years—it's GONE.

The older Michael Jackson, whose *Off the Wall* and *Thriller* albums dominated the soundtrack to my years in Destrehan, Louisiana (1978–1986)—GONE.

In the past month, memories of my childhood and youth died off: first Ed, then Farrah, then Michael.

Last weekend I drove through the parishes along the Mississippi River in which I was raised, and then up into Bogue Chitto, Mississippi, and relived some great memories, telling my two sons about it all and meeting up with lifelong friends and family—but those days are all GONE.

The Teacher in Ecclesiastes writes, "Vanity of vanities! All is vanity," and, "The people long ago are not remembered, nor will there be any remembrance of people yet to come by those who come after them."

I know the Teacher is right. In the grand scheme of things, the Teacher is absolutely right. But in the little blip of time that is my life, remembering is anything *but* vanity. It is a shaping and guiding presence. Of course, I can remember simple facts: I remember that 1 + 1 = 2; that on December 1, 1973, the Tulane Green Wave broke a two-decade losing streak against their archrival LSU Tigers; and that Lew DeWitt was one of the four original Statler Brothers.

But the passing of people, places, and things is more than that kind of factual memory; it's mystical and experiential. Just mentioning the names Ed McMahon, Farrah Fawcett, and Michael Jackson will bring to life for me thousands of memories, sights, sounds, scents, family, and friends. I thank God for that powerful presence through which the things that are gone continue to live.

Of God, Oral Roberts, and Mrs. Brabham

Televangelist Oral Roberts had just died, and his death brought back a lot of memories, specifically about one person.

Mrs. Barbara Brabham taught me ninth grade English in Jefferson Parish, Louisiana, and she was one of the most joy-filled people I've ever met.

She was also living with the effects of having polio as a young girl: a disproportionate body with small, unstable legs. She walked around school with a satchel full of books and papers hung around her shoulders, and with the assistance of silver polio crutches—those crutches with cuffs that reach around and secure themselves to the forearms, with bicycle hand grips.

Honestly, I don't remember a lot of what she taught us about Charles Dickens, but I do remember talking about Fleetwood Mac, Jethro Tull, Keith Green, and Larry Norman during lunch breaks and off-periods. And I remember talking about church and faith . . . and polio.

Mrs. Brabham introduced me to the charismatic movement within Christianity. The charismatic movement, with its dancing, hand-raising, tongue-speaking, and passionate, emotional music, was a perfect fit for a young "proper Baptist" kid who loved Jesus, but who also loved to rock out with the Beatles, Led Zeppelin, and Lynyrd Skynyrd (back in the early years just after the plane crash, when Skynyrd was—for the time being, at least—no more).

Because Mrs. Brabham was a teenager in the early-to-mid seventies, she knew all the great rock groups that I loved, and she had even seen some of them in concert. I hung around Mrs. Brabham a lot during my freshman year just to hear her stories, which she would always bring around to her faith in Jesus. At a critical point in my early teen years, when I was trying to decide if I wanted to be a good "Christian" (at that time, this meant being a "proper, upstanding, clean-cut" Baptist) or a wild rock-and-roll rebel, Mrs. Brabham was one of two individuals whom God placed in my path to remind me that rebelling against boredom and institutional religion was one thing; but I didn't need to confuse God with the things against which I was rebelling.

Many adults I knew in the Baptist church were worried about my record collection and about my rock-and-roll t-shirts and posters. Mrs. Brabham, though, never judged me and never criticized my taste in music or my preference for ripped jeans and shirts. Instead, she spoke my language. She listened, smiled, shared her stories, and then introduced me to the "Jesus music" that she was listening to. Those folks had long hair, some played loud guitars, and they all sang about their faith in the culture that they knew—which was far outside the traditional church walls.

Once the conversation turned to Oral Roberts. Another classmate and I were probably making jokes about him (as I was frequently apt to do); by this time he had already amassed a fortune and had seen a 900-foot-tall Jesus.

Mrs. Brabham shared that when she was younger, her father took her to an Oral Roberts healing service. Obviously, she was neither cured nor spared the lasting effects of polio. Yet, Mrs. Brabham did not hold that against God. She had come to terms with her physical body; she had "accepted the cards she had been dealt" (as card players say); and her faith in and love for God were not contingent on whether God made her "perfect," healthy, and wealthy.

What I found most unbelievable, though, was that she didn't speak ill of Oral Roberts! I wanted her to mock him. I wanted her to say that the faith of her father and her own faith was good enough for God, even if it wasn't good enough for Oral to heal her. I wanted her to say Oral was a fraud, a prophet of a false gospel, or, in the words of Will Campbell, a "soul molester."

But the fact was that Mrs. Brabham *liked* Oral Roberts—as hard as that was for me to accept. Today, her son is a graduate of Oral Roberts University.

I cannot overemphasize the influence Mrs. Brabham had on my faith, and in my life, during my freshman year. God used her to accept me and affirm me as a rock-and-roll misfit, but also to challenge and strengthen me in my walk with Christ.

I am by no means a fan of "prosperity gospel" evangelists. And it's hard for me *not* to speak critically of the lifestyle, teachings, and claims of someone like Oral Roberts. But could I broaden my theology enough to accept that despite my convictions, God could still use Oral Roberts?

After all, I *believe* God spoke to Balaam through an ass (that's a donkey for you non-King James folks). I *know* God has spoken to me through Mick Jagger (that's another story). And I *hope* that—maybe even once or twice—God has spoken to somebody through me.

Because I love and trust Mrs. Brabham, I know that despite my feelings to the contrary, God has spoken to at least one person through Oral Roberts.

Hippy-Dippy Youth Ministry

(Ode to Jimmie Knox, Jr.)

We all knew Jimmie Knox, Jr., as "Little Jimmie." His dad, "Brother Jimmie" Knox, was the pastor who baptized my sister and me at First Baptist Church, Norco, Louisiana.

Little Jimmie was the paid part-time youth minister. He had another full-time job, of course. I don't recall what that was, if I ever even knew.

When I was ten years old, my family moved to St. Charles Parish, and we began attending FBC Norco. My sister, going into high school, was immediately welcomed into the youth group; I had to watch from the sidelines. I couldn't *wait* to get into seventh grade—not because of school, but because I couldn't wait to get into the youth group.

It was a small but active youth. Little Jimmie and his wife, Linda, organized swimming parties, Sunday night fellowships and devotionals, movie nights, Centrifuge summer youth trips, and rides into nearby Kenner, Metairie, and LaPlace for pizza.

Little Jimmie had organized the youth group into the excellent "Sonshine Players" puppet team. The Sonshine Players were good . . . *very* good.

Jimmie and Linda understood the discipline and art of puppetry. FBC Norco had quality puppets. Lots of costumes. A well-made stage with thick curtains. And a pretty good portable sound system.

Youth practiced throughout the week—walking around with their puppet arms extended up next to their heads and into the air for long periods of time, constantly assuming the proper puppet position and exercising their thumbs while keeping their hands and fingers as still as possible.

And they went on tour: the Sonshine Players performed puppet shows on the Florida beach and in churches along whatever routes they took on trips.

By the time I got into the youth group, the older youth (including my sister) were all graduating; the puppet team was dwindling and losing its critical mass. Also about that time, Brother Jimmie resigned to minister elsewhere, and with him went Little Jimmie and Linda.

But in my one short year in "his" youth group, Little Jimmie planted important seeds that would take deep root and begin to grow under the next several youth ministers (I had five different youth ministers between seventh and twelfth grades).

Little Jimmie introduced me to "Christian" music that was unlike anything I had ever heard: most notably the soundtrack to *Godspell.* Since I was already developing a deep fondness for Woodstock and all things hippy, *Godspell* was talking to me in my language. Likewise, he introduced me to the music of Gary S. Paxton (don't forget the "S."; that's one-third of his whole name!). Many times Little Jimmie loaned me his *Godspell* and Gary S. Paxton cassette tapes; I memorized all the songs on both albums, and Little Jimmie and I would quote them and sing them to each other.

He also loved to laugh. He gave (not loaned, but *gave*) me two of his old comedy albums, which I still have: the Smothers Brothers' classic *Mom Always Liked You Best!* and the brilliant *Take-Offs and Put-Ons* by the not-yet-FCC-foe George Carlin. Little Jimmie and I would take turns trading Smothers Brothers' lines and quoting Carlin's entire "Al Sleet, the Hippy-Dippy Weatherman" skit.

Little Jimmie also taught me that good people get divorced.

In the 1970s and early 1980s, Southern Baptists preached a lot about divorce, leaving me as a young pre-teenager with the impression that divorce was essentially an *unforgivable sin* in God's eyes.

When my family arrived at Norco, I had to face perhaps my first serious theological crisis—a man I loved and respected was *divorced* (Linda was Little Jimmie's second wife). A man leading and teaching youth, praying for and with youth, singing and praying in church . . . and the preacher's *son*, no less! It took a bit of wrestling, but in my early pre-teenage years, I had to admit that I didn't understand everything in the Bible, and that the harsh preachers quoting it had obviously never met Little Jimmie and Linda.

I had not heard from or about Little Jimmie (or any of the Knoxes) for more than two decades. On a recent trek through Norco, some of my FBC church family informed me that Little Jimmie had died.

As an adult, I never got to tell Little Jimmie how much his short-lived presence in my life meant to me; maybe somehow by God's grace this musing will find its way into the hands of Linda or even Brother Jimmie—wherever they may be.

But to Little Jimmie, who taught me (in the words of Gary S. Paxton) that "there's got to be more to livin', than people just waitin' to die," I love you. Thank you for your ministry to me when I needed it most. And anytime I watch *Godspell* or share Smothers Brothers' stories with others, I always remember you.

Until then, Little Jimmie, this is Bert Montgomery, your hippy-dippy weatherman, with all the hippy, dippy weather . . . *man* . . . .

Of Plane Fares and Providence

(Ode to Pat McCormick)

Providence.

I don't believe in some freaky puppet master yanking on strings and making everything happen, but I do believe God is actively involved in our lives and our world, weaving things together for some holy purpose. Strange and unexplainable things sometimes happen, and when they do, we often call it "coincidence." I prefer to leave open the possibility that God's Providence may be at work.

Like how on a Monday afternoon in August, my wife Jency found a $400 Delta Airlines voucher lying around that was going to expire in September. Last September, I got "bumped" by Delta and given the voucher to make up for it—they do that sort of thing when they overbook flights, and then I did what any self-respecting man would do: I placed the voucher somewhere and forgot about it. Until a few weeks ago on a Monday afternoon when my wife just happened to see it.

Like how that same Monday evening I had this sense, this gut feeling, that I should call my old friend Kate McCormick. I dug around a little bit, found Kate's cell phone number, and left her a message. "Kate, we love you and are praying for you and your family," I said.

When I first met Kate, she was a leader in the youth group at First United Methodist Church, Henderson, Kentucky. Kate is now in her mid-twenties, an accomplished and respected musician, and on that Monday when I called her, she was at home in Henderson caring for her parents: her father, Pat, dying of cancer, and her mother, Heather, living with an inoperable brain tumor.

Tuesday was just another normal day for me. Wednesday morning, though, I received word that Pat had passed away Tuesday evening. Visitation would be on Friday evening there in Henderson, and the memorial service would be Saturday at noon at First Methodist.

I called Jency to let her know. "You have to try to go," she said.

So less than forty-eight hours from the time Jency found the $400 Delta Airlines voucher, I was searching for plane fares to Evansville, Indiana (just a few minutes' drive from Henderson). It was a $405 round-trip, provided I fly out on Friday and back on Sunday.

Off I went and spent two nights at the house of some friends of ours. It was good to celebrate Pat's life and to grieve with old friends who have played, and continue to play, such an important part in my faith journey.

So Jency found a soon-to-expire voucher; I was mysteriously urged to call Kate; Pat passed away; and I redeemed the aforementioned voucher for a weekend of grief and celebration in Henderson, Kentucky. And I was reminded of just how important those brief eight months I lived in Henderson, some seven years ago, still are to my family and me.

Coincidence? You may think so.

I'll go with Providence.

Dear Richard—Goodbye, Farewell, and Amen

(Ode to Richard Delisi)

February 2009. Suicide is NOT painless . . . .

The first song I heard when I turned on the car radio was "Tunnel," the Third Day song proclaiming,

> There's a light at the end of this tunnel
> Shinin' bright at the end of this tunnel
> For you, for you
> So keep holdin' on.[1]

That's the honest truth.

I just got off the phone with a total stranger, the sister of an old friend and former next-door neighbor of ours. She found old letters from us, and our phone number, in Richard's rented duplex and decided she should notify us. Richard, our one-time Memphis neighbor and our friend for about twelve years, committed suicide this week.

I got in the car to pick my up my wife and to inform her of the bad news, and *this* Third Day song was playing on the radio.

While I normally really like the song, and it speaks to me and other friends who often try to ward off deep depression, all I could say was, "Well, that light just didn't shine quite brightly enough for Richard to hold on any longer."

Music was essential to Richard—it was ingrained in his soul. And so music has been speaking to me (or haunting me) for the past twenty-four hours since I received the call. Ironically, it has not been Richard's music, per se. Richard loved simple three-or-four-piece jazz ensembles. He played bass guitar. And he loved the Beatles. When we were next-door neighbors (very *close* next door neighbors with only a single-car driveway between our side doors), I could hear Beatles or jazz music playing any time he was home.

But instead, songs about pain, despair, and suicide have been on my mind. Like this one from Simon and Garfunkel:

> He died last Saturday
> He turned on the gas and he went to sleep
> with the windows closed so he'd never wake up
> to his silent world and his tiny room . . . .[2]

That was Richard. In some ways the whole song is Richard. While we knew and loved Richard—he was so gentle, caring, and selfless—he was also a solitary and self-described "lonely" man. And that's exactly what he did: he closed himself off in a small room and released some gas so he'd never wake up to his lonely and silent world.

Then there's this song from Kate Campbell:

> if the heart is a bottomless pit, you gotta watch what you put in it
> How much can one heart hold?
> Before you know it you're carrying around, a ton of stuff that'll
> weigh you down
> How much can one heart hold?[3]

Richard came to see us not quite two weeks ago. We went out to eat and talked about classic movies (he was excited that we're raising our children on Hitchcock and Jimmy Stewart and Frank Capra). We showed him around Starkville, hoping we could help him find a job here, and that he would stay with us until he got back on his feet. But as we talked privately, it was obvious his heart was carrying around so much pain and hurt and rejection, and no matter how much we and another friend tried to help carry his weight, his heart just couldn't hold any more.

He and I went out for coffee while he was here. After some tears and a lot of despair, something spurred us into a conversation about George Carlin and Richard Pryor. Richard began to laugh. He laughed *hard*. We shared favorite Carlin and Pryor quotes with each other and spoke of the deep insights of the two comedians. He became animated as he told stories. It was a moment of pure grace.

But it didn't last long.

He came on a Friday night and left before we could buy him lunch on Sunday. There was something about the way he hugged each of us—long, tight hugs, with a heartfelt expression of "thank you"; and he eased away, looked deep into our eyes, and said, "goodbye."

I think, then, I knew.

We called our mutual friend in Memphis who was having daily contact with Richard—buying him groceries, inviting him over for dinner, even trying to help him admit himself into a hospital. We called our friend, Dan, and told him that Richard had left our house and was heading back to Memphis. Dan continued that regular and deeply caring contact for the next week and a half (even calling and leaving Richard a message on his answering machine about a job fair on the same day Richard's sister called me).

My family and I have been watching a lot of *M*A*S*H* episodes together, and the theme song is appropriate (the words are sung in the movie version):

> The sword of time will pierce our skins
> It doesn't hurt when it begins
> But as it works its way on in
> The pain grows stronger, watch it grin
> Suicide is painless.[4]

I'm at least thankful that for Richard, with all the pain and sorrow and loneliness that all seemed to grin as they were destroying him, his suicide was painless. He is finally a soul at rest and peace.

And lest anyone express judgment upon Richard, think about these words from Frederick Buechner, a minister and author (I advise reading as much Buechner as you can):

Taking your own life is not mentioned as a sin in the Bible. There's no suggestion that it was considered either shameful or cowardly. When, as in the case of Saul and Judas, pain, horror, and despair reach a certain point, suicide is perhaps less a voluntary act than a reflex action. If you're being burned alive with a loaded pistol in your hand, it's hard to see how anyone can seriously hold it against you for pulling the trigger.

Notes

1. *Wherever You Are*, Essential, 2005.

2. "A Most Peculiar Man," *Sounds of Silence*, Columbia Records, 1966.

3. "How Much Can One Heart Hold," *Monuments*, Large River Music, 2001.

4. Johnny Mandel and Mike Altman, "Song from M*A*S*H* (Suicide is Painless)," Columbia/CBS Records, 1970.

5. Frederick Buechner, *Whistling in the Dark: A Doubter's Dictionary* (San Francisco: HarperSanFrancisco: 1993) 115–16.

Part 2

Because God's Ways Are *Not* Our Ways

because we look at the outside, but God looks at the heart
because in Christ there is no Jew nor Greek,
no "insured" nor "uninsured,"
no "legal" nor "illegal,"
no "_____" nor "_____" (you fill in the blanks)
because in Christ there are only people created in God's image
for whom Jesus died and for whom Jesus rose again

Of Pea Pods and Hurricanes

(*Owed* to Ellen DeGeneres, and to Renee and Connie)

The following musing was composed in September 2005 while I was a student at the Baptist Seminary of Kentucky. It was based on a news report that Pat Robertson publicly declared Hurricane Katrina was God's judgment upon New Orleans because Ellen DeGeneres is gay. That news report was quickly pulled (but not until after I wrote my thoughts) when it was discovered to be a piece of satire not based on fact. However, as even snopes.com acknowledges, there wasn't much (if any) exaggeration involved to suggest Pat Robertson would say such a thing—Brother Pat is unfortunately fond of publicly pronouncing God's judgment in the aftermath of disasters and tragedies.

In June 2009, my Mississippi College friend Renee and her partner spoke briefly at the Annual United Methodist Conference in Mississippi. They spoke of a particular congregation that has welcomed them, loved them, and helped nurture them in their faith. Understandably, their testimony created a bit of a stir. While I support dialogue and civil disagreement, and, technically, I "don't have a dog in this fight" (I'm a Baptist, not a Methodist, minister), I will not remain quiet while some people openly question the integrity and the faith of a friend.

So, acknowledging that the basis of this musing is actually fictional (Pat Robertson never really said this, but again, see snopes.com for similar remarks he actually has said), I maintain that the spirit of this piece and the message I intended to convey are relevant and truthful.

The Reverend Pat Robertson and I have a lot in common. We both hail from and still live in the South—I'm from Louisiana and now live in Kentucky; Pat's from and still lives in Virginia.

We both value higher education—I like classrooms so much I'm working on a second master's degree; Pat values education so much he *owns* an institution of higher learning. I live in a state that races valuable horses; Pat breeds valuable racehorses. And, as if that weren't enough, Pat Robertson and I are both ordained Baptist ministers. Yep, me and Pat, Pat and me: like two peas from the same pod.

It just so happens that I also have a lot in common with Ellen DeGeneres. Ellen enjoys having her own television shows; I enjoy watching Ellen's television shows. Ellen's brother, Vance DeGeneres, used to be in a rock band called The Cold; I once saw Ellen's brother, Vance, play with his rock band The Cold. And, as if TV and rock n' roll weren't enough, Ellen DeGeneres and I were both born and raised in the New Orleans area. Yep—me and Ellen, Ellen and me: like two peas from the same pod.

But then that would make Pat and Ellen from the same pod, too, wouldn't it?

I read somewhere that Pat blamed Ellen for Hurricane Katrina (say it ain't so, Pat!). I guess it's a stretch to think that Ellen and Pat share a pea pod.

I wish I could help these peas get together. I wish I could get Ellen to . . . convince Ellen to . . . well, Ellen's not really at fault here as far as I can tell.

So I've got to address Pat. I'm worried about us, Pat—two Baptist preachers from the Southland. I'm worried because I read the Gospels, and it is clear that Jesus saves his judgment for the religious leaders— good, upstanding, righteous folks who feel they are too "good" to love others, too "good" to serve others, too "good" to be friends with others. Jesus saves his words of judgment for those religious folks who are so "good" that they freely pass judgment on others who aren't "good enough."

It's really quite simple, Pat: Jesus has a whole lot to say about money, power, arrogance, and self-righteousness, but doggone that Savior of ours, he never says one blasted word about sexual orientation. Not one! Go look it up for yourself.

Yes, I've got hang-ups and concerns—we all do. But Pat, I've got to take this into serious consideration, because, after all, I'm called to be like Jesus. And Jesus spends more time hanging out with, having fun with, living among, and loving the real people in the world—people who are not "good enough" by religious leaders' standards—than he does with religious leaders who have high opinions of themselves. And don't ever forget, Pat, it's religious leaders like us who led the charge to execute our Lord.

Pat, all I'm going by are your public statements, but your declarations seem pretentious, arrogant, and self-righteous. Besides, Pat, with all that wealth you've accumulated from your television station, your TV ministry, your books, your horses, and, let's not forget, your fascination with political power, it's easy to imagine Jesus having a few choice words for you as he walks off to enjoy a cup of coffee with Ellen.

Pat, I love you, my brother, my pea-pod-sharing friend, but I'm choosing to follow Jesus on this one. And if I hurry, I might be able to catch up with him and Ellen. I sure hope they have some chicory at that coffee shop . . . .

Sin, Salvation, and Johnny Cash

In October 2008, I was invited by the festival coordinator to speak on redemption at the 2nd Annual Pardon Johnny Cash Flower Pickin' Festival in Starkville, Mississippi. This is what I said.

I don't know about you, but just about everything I know about sin, salvation, and redemption I learned from Johnny Cash.

That's not really true. I mean, I did grow up in church and I did go to seminary and all, and I'm sure I may have learned some things along the way, but it sounds right (and it's not too far from the truth) to say that just about everything I know about sin, salvation, and redemption I learned from Johnny Cash.

Allow me to read from our Scriptures this evening . . . well, not directly from our Scriptures, but the echoes of our Scriptures through the voice of Johnny Cash via the Gospel according to Tom Waits:

There's a place I know where the train goes slow
Where the sinner can be washed in the blood of the lamb
There's a river by the trestle down by sinner's grove
Down where the willow and the dogwood grow

You can hear the whistle, you can hear the bell
From the halls of heaven to the gates of hell
And there's room for the forsaken if you're there on time
You'll be washed of all your sins and all of your crimes
If you're down there by the train

Down there by the train, Down there by the train
Down there by the train, Down there where the train goes slow[1]

You know about Johnny Cash. You know the stories of his reck-
lessness and brokenness. That's part of why we're here tonight. You
know the stories of his redemption and healing. That's what we're celebrating tonight. You know of his close friendship with the Reverend
Billy Graham, and of his infamous prison concerts. If you don't know
why he always wore black, search online for Cash's song "Man in
Black." You'll be glad you did.

But you may or may not know about this: The story goes that
when convicted murderer Gary Gilmore was sentenced to be executed
back in 1976, after hearing that Gilmore was a longtime fan of his,
Johnny Cash sent Gilmore a copy of his autobiography, *The Man in
Black*, and he later called Gilmore on death row to speak to him before
his execution by a firing squad.[2]

I'm certain Cash wasn't cold-hearted and indifferent to the families
of Gilmore's victims and their pain, but neither was Cash indifferent
to the personal pain and uncontrolled anger that can put a man on
death row. Cash, more than just about any preacher I know, was able
to extend mercy to the merciless, love the unlovable, and offer the
hope of redemption to those most of us mark off as far beyond
redemption.

I suspect Johnny knew deeper than most of us that if God could
love him, with all of his excesses and faults and extremes—"such a
worm as I," he sings in the old hymn—then God could love anybody,
even a cold-hearted murderer.

And that's why I say that just about everything I know about sin,
salvation, and redemption I learned from Johnny Cash.

But don't take my word for it. Listen to these other holy words of
redemption that Cash so earnestly sang to us:

Well, I've never asked forgiveness and I've never said a prayer
Never given of myself, never truly cared
I've left the ones who loved me and I'm still raising Cain
I've taken the low road and if you've done the same

Meet me down there by the train
Down there by the train, Down there by the train
Down there by the train, Down there where the train goes slow

Thanks be to God for the songs of Johnny Cash, and for his life that both received and so freely gave away God's most amazing grace!

Notes

1. Tom Waits, "Down There by the Train," Johnny Cash's *American Recordings*, American/Sony Records, 1994.

2. You can read all about Gary Gilmore, including the Johnny Cash connection, and learn sociology, too, from younger brother Mikal Gilmore's haunting memoir, *Shot in the Heart* (New York: Doubleday, 1994).

Helter Skelter and Amazing Grace

(Jesus Loves You, Charlie Manson)

I clearly remember buying Vincent Bugliosi's now legendary book *Helter Skelter* in paperback from my local grocery store when I was about twelve years old. I spent many hot summer days in St. Charles Parish, Louisiana, spread out on my comfortable bed in my air-conditioned room, captivated by Bugliosi's story. It wasn't too long before the made-for-TV movie made it's occasional airing, and then I saw that, too.

I guess this was the beginning of my sociological imagination. I have always wondered, what can make a little kid grow up and commit murder? And in the case of the Manson family, what can make little kids grow up, become obsessed with a crazed madman, and then commit such unspeakable acts of violence and torture? Following those questions, one more followed: what can make a little boy grow up into a crazed madman with such hatred and paranoia and mental instabilities that he would recruit young followers and then convince them to carry out his apocalyptic biddings?

I remember pondering all these things at that young age, and I remember asking, is there anything keeping *me* from falling into such traps? After all, some of Manson's "family" were good school kids, middle-class kids, even *church* kids. Then I began looking around at people I knew at school and in the neighborhood, and they weren't very different from some of the family members who had a rough life growing up and found somebody who would take them in unconditionally.

I guess what I am getting at is that I am a murderer, too. That's hard for me to say. I have never stabbed anybody, shot anybody, or poisoned anybody; nor have I ever tried. I'm actually a bit of an easy-going pacifist.

But I have really been filled with hatred toward a person or two before. I have *really* wished I could turn into the Hulk and beat somebody to a pulp who was bullying me. I have imagined how much nicer the world would be if a few people didn't exist anymore.

And I've heard Jesus say to me, then, that I have committed murder in my heart. So who am I to judge?

I saw the most recent 2009 mug shot of Charles Manson on a news website. Even in not-too-long-ago prison mug shots, Manson still gave off bad vibes—he continued to convey hatred, venom, almost pure evil in his stare. But this shot was different. The swastika still permanently scars his forehead, but apart from that, he's an old, sad-looking man.

I still hurt for the many families who have been forever tortured by Manson's actions and his memory. And I also hurt for the families who had to endure the news that a child they loved—a son, daughter, brother, sister, cousin, nephew, or niece—had committed heinous crimes and would spend the rest of his or her life in jail.

But, for the first time ever, I felt pity for Manson when I saw this picture. I tried not to, but I couldn't help it. Because underneath the swastika, and underneath the twisted paranoid hallucinations, and beneath the hatred—before there was a madman with a messianic complex; before there was a violent adult seducing young hippies with lots of drugs and sex; before there was a frustrated singer who couldn't get a record deal, years and years before all of those things—there was a little boy and an angry world around him. And now, there's an old, pathetic, pitiful man, and a still angry world around him.

I kind of felt like he's that sorry, old uncle we all have—you know, the mean drunk that most people despised and nobody in the family could tolerate much, though occasionally we *might* recall a glimpse of goodness in his heart.

I remember hearing a preacher ask a long time ago, "If God is love, and grace is real, then what about somebody like Charles Manson?"

And for the first time, I think I understand what that preacher was trying to say.

Singing "Father Abraham" for Peace

September 2009. May God forgive us for our intentional ignorance.

As a child growing up in the church, I learned the cute little children's song "Father Abraham" (and its corresponding physical movements):

> Father Abraham had many sons,
> many sons had Father Abraham
> I am one of them and so are you,
> so let's just praise the Lord!
> Right arm! Left arm! . . .

This year we marked the eighth year since the 9/11 terrorist attacks on our nation; attacks that have led some to view Islam as the enemy of Christianity; much as in other lands some see Jews as the enemy of Muslims.

On the evening of September 10, 2009, I attended an interfaith dialogue on Mississippi State's campus. In stark contrast to stereotypes, we all sat together—representatives of Judaism, Islam, and Christianity—and not one person was hurt. In fact, the entire evening was peaceful and a call to focus on our commonalities.

Which brings me back to that cute little children's song that has stuck with me as I've grown older; and perhaps that cute little children's song isn't such a cute little children's song after all, but a song of profound truth for God's children of all ages.

The reason some folks don't care much for other folks in other faith traditions is *not* out of allegiance to some great religious truth, but out of allegiance to political, military, and cultural forces that may have claimed the name of some great religious truth. They are operating in ignorance of the religious truths they claim to defend.

In other words, we could all use a refresher course in introduction to religion, particularly as it relates to the three great monotheistic traditions of the world. Christians respect the Jewish Scriptures and add a New Testament. Muslims respect the Jewish and Christian Scriptures and add the Qur'an.

We *all* tell the stories of Moses, David, and the prophets.

And we *all* pray to and praise the God of Abraham.

Now there are significant differences, practices, and traditions, to be sure. But the three great monotheistic faiths of the world proclaim *one* God, the Creator of all that is, and God is a God of love, compassion, justice, and peace. From there our unique experiences, teachings, and practices go in all sorts of directions shaped—for good and for ill—by territories, experiences, cultures, and even politics and economics.

But can we respect each other's differences and unique traditions while celebrating our common ancestry? Sure we can.

At first glance, an outsider could easily assume that my parents have little, if anything, in common with me; in fact, we could easily stand in total contrast and even opposition to each other. When I was a child, my parents took my sister and me to a performance by Lawrence Welk, his orchestra, and everyone else associated with his show. I responded by becoming a die-hard KISS fan before I even hit the preteen years. My parents still prefer the clean-cut, presentable look; I wear an earring and I prefer longer, scraggly hair.

In 1974, we spent one evening of our family vacation in a hotel room watching President Richard Nixon resign; my parents cried. Even as early as 1972, at only four years old, I think I knew I was going to be a McGovern kind of guy.

In spite of our many tremendous differences in terms of values, beliefs, politics, and concert preferences, my family and I also have a lot in common. We share great life experiences, strong emotional bonds, and, of course, genes. I love my family and they love me. And these days, when we get together, I treasure every moment and have learned to respect and appreciate our differences.

My parents and I share our faith tradition, but even there we find lots of differences. I think my parents prefer the nuggets of wisdom found in the Proverbs. I prefer the existential angst of Ecclesiastes. I think my parents have a natural lean toward Paul's epistles; I am naturally inclined toward the book of James.

But I'll never forget that they raised me in my faith and taught me about God. And in the church of my parents, I learned the song "Father Abraham."

Which brings me back to Muslims, Jews, and Christians—all of us who trace our lineage directly back to Abraham and to the God of Abraham.

Maybe we should sponsor some sort of interfaith sing-along in a public place, inviting more and more people around us to join in, each of us wearing the symbols of our particular traditions, but in a huge circle dancing and singing and celebrating together:

> Father Abraham had many sons,
> many sons had Father Abraham
> I am one of them and so are you,
> so let's just praise the Lord!

It may seem a bit hokey, but it is far more faithful to the God we claim to worship than blowing each other up.

Holy Health Care, Batman!

(First Thoughts)

Written August 2009 because it's an abomination that in one of the richest, most advanced societies in the history of the world, with such a large presence of the Christian tradition, health care is an expensive luxury enjoyed by a shrinking few.

I write from a perspective of faith. Sometimes I write in broad, general terms, but today I am writing to all in who identify themselves as Christians. To the pastors and teachers, bishops and priests, deacons and elders, and to all who enter church doors week after week, let us affirm a common belief: each and every person is created in the image of God.

In our nation full of churches; in our nation where some churches have budgets the size of a small state; in our nation where we Christians, regardless of church size, proclaim that all life is sacred, let's talk with each other about health care.

Pundits yell back and forth about it on television. Newspaper columnists weigh in on it daily. Politicians debate it in Washington, D.C. Friends argue about it over cups of coffee.

Yet the dangerously radical proclamation of the holiness of all human life may be the rallying point on which the gazillions of churches in America can focus. Maybe it can even bring the hundreds of thousands of divided churches in our nation together, and maybe we can be the starting point for the rest of the country.

We sit by and allow others to argue while men, women, and countless children are denied access to health care because their lives are *not* considered as sacred, but rather as game pieces to be shuffled around by money managers.

Please hear me out: I am not about being a Republican or Democrat, capitalist or socialist, doctor or patient. I am not talking about lobbyists, insurance companies, hospital interests, or congressional debates.

I don't care about the politics. I am talking about people of faith doing something that matters. I'm talking about backing up our words with action.

In some larger cities, a few churches have joined together with doctors and nurses and other medical folks and have started health clinics to serve their communities. This care is free if need be, or is offered for fees to those who can afford to pay. Everybody, rich or poor, old or young, gets seen and cared for as a ministry of the area churches.

I don't know what the political and economical answer is to our health care situation in this country. But while everyone argues over interests and monies and control, maybe it's time we as the church start practicing what we preach—that people are not viewed as "insured" or "uninsured" or "preexisting conditions" or anything else, but as human beings worthy of care because they are created in God's image, and because we proclaim the holiness, the sacredness, of human life.

Can we find creative ways to join with other congregations in our communities, counties, and states—working together with the doctors and nurses and hospital staff in our congregations—to care for one another as if our lives really are holy and worth something (like Acts and others Scriptures dare to proclaim)?

Let's face it, the health care solution will not come from bureaucrats in high-rise office buildings, from politicians in the chambers of Congress, from doctors, nurses, insurance CEOs, or hospital board members, or from legions of patients' interests groups. They will do what they will do, sometimes for better and sometimes for worse.

But no matter what our social institutions choose to do (or not do), the church has something to offer to the world—the radical gospel message that each person's life, regardless of socioeconomic status, means something; that each person's life is worth caring for because each person bears the image of God.

Health care is not just a political issue or a financial issue. From a Christian perspective, health care is a moral issue. So while powers and interests argue and fight with each other, let the churches right here in the Golden Triangle Region begin to speak. Let the churches right here in this region of Mississippi—Pentecostals, Methodists, Lutherans, Presbyterians, Disciples of Christ, Baptists, Episcopalians, Catholics, and so on and so forth—begin to act.

We declare not just by word, but by deed, that every life is holy and deserves love and care. All the elderly. All the children. The working poor. The working rich. The lazy in every group.

The president. The governor. The senators and representatives. The upper class. The lower class. The middle class. Even those who have no class.

The deserving. The undeserving. The most important. The *least of these*.

Everyone is created in God's own image.

How can we pay for it? To paraphrase Will Campbell—a Mississippi-born-and-bred Baptist preacher—the same way we afford our steeples, family life centers, staff salaries, lighted crosses, and so on . . . with our tithes and offerings.

With tithes and offerings—for the glory of God and for the love of others. What can be more Christian than that?

Gospel Care

(Second Thoughts)

Also written in August 2009 because it truly is an abomination that in one of the richest, most advanced societies in the history of the world, where so many of us are so proud and loud about our Christian faith, we don't practice basic Christian values when it comes to caring for each other.

During the two weeks that followed the original publication of the previous "Holy Health Care, Batman!" article, it was picked up and carried in a few other places. Something about it spoke to people.

Responses ranged from that of a Baptist friend, who happens to be a physician, reminding me that government-run health care (i.e., Medicare/Medicaid) is already a bureaucratic nightmare, and that expanding it will just make it worse for everybody; to another Baptist friend, who also happens to be a physician, reminding me that it is the government's responsibility to protect and provide for its citizens.

Then there was a response from a Methodist friend who is ready to jump in and get moving on what she termed "Gospel Care." She may be on to something.

After all, were the Methodist hospitals and Baptist hospitals and Catholic hospitals in our cities originally established as money-making machines? Of course not. They were established to provide needed medical care for communities, especially during epidemics and other major health crises. And why was that? Because we proclaimed that, by God, every life is sacred and worthy of care, and so, by God, we Christians would care for each other and our communities.

But a tragic thing happened to our missions activities: they became businesses. Our Methodist and Baptist and Catholic hospitals now operate to serve a board of directors; to care for the "bottom line"; to obey the commandments of insurance companies. What were once missions for the love of God and others have become institutions competing for dollars.

Every year we in our American churches organize medical mission trips and travel all over the world to provide medical care for people who do not have access to it. We do this because God calls us to do so. Here at home, though, we surrender our calling to businesses and government, and we watch as millions and millions of people continue to be denied access to medical care.

One Wednesday evening I sat in a living room with fellow Christians, and I listened to a story about two women who, some fifty or so years ago, went into North Africa proclaiming that God loves anybody and everybody, and that there is nobody who stands beyond God's love. The people there corrected them—God did *not* love at least one group of people: illegitimate children.

Illegitimate children were not loved by God, and therefore not to be loved by others. Boys were tossed into the deserts to die; girls were sold to become slaves. These two women stood firm and said, "No. God *does* love them. Give them to us. We will care for them." They took in babies, infants, and young children. They fed them, clothed them, educated them, and raised them as people of worth simply because they were God's children, too.

To my fellow Christians at all levels of society (especially those in business, in insurance, and in health care professions), our actions are saying that some people are *not* loved by God, and therefore do not need to be loved by us. The gods of money and profit and efficiency are willing to toss people aside, and we are allowing it to happen.

We have lost our prophetic voice, which should be declaring to these false gods, "No! God *does* love them. Give them to us. We will care for them."

As we begin to care for those "not good enough" for the gods of commerce, we will discover that we are caring for ourselves in the process. We are all people of worth simply because we are God's children.

St. Jude Children's Research Hospital in Memphis, which has an outstanding reputation for research and treatment, will care for any child who comes through its doors, regardless of ability to pay.

So, to those running Christian-named hospitals and clinics that were established as missions, let's obey our Lord's teachings; let's be consistent in our beliefs and actions; and let's simply treat anybody and everybody who comes through our doors with the best research-based treatment available, regardless of income or insurance.

We don't have to wait for the government to bureaucratize everything, and we don't have to wait for CEOs of insurance companies to stop trying to get out of paying for treatments so they can pocket more cash. We just need to agree that this is who we are as people of faith, and we will care for each other and our communities because God loves everyone.

St. Jude does it for sick children. We *used* to do it for anybody.

Let's take our names back from the gods of commerce and return our names and our efforts to the work of God's kingdom.

Gospel care. We've done it before, and we can do it again. As Will Campbell reminds us, we can do it with our tithes and offerings, and with our hearts filled with God's love for all God's children.

Reality Show Redemption: WWJD?

It's a tale of two "men of God"—one sent to preach repentance and to proclaim the coming of the Lord, and the other, well, sent to be the Lord.

Sure there were some similarities between them:

1. they shared a bloodline (they were cousins);
2. both were born of women who shouldn't have been pregnant to begin with;
3. and they were most certainly *not* the white-skinned folks in the Sunday school pictures I grew up seeing.

But these may be all the similarities. When it came to their messages, to their behavior, and to the people with whom they associated, there weren't many similarities at all.

John the Baptizer would have been a great judge on a reality TV show. Jesus, not so much.

We like it when our prophets start ripping people to shreds for their shortcomings and failures. We feel great glee when someone's bubble bursts, when someone gets humiliated for trying to be what others want them to be.

We want our prophets to be like *American Idol*'s Simon Cowell—watching people do their best to try to win his vote only to tear into them, point out their imperfections, and tell them why they will never amount to much of anything.

We want our prophets to be like Donald Trump. After all, it's nothing personal: business is business and faith is faith. Either you get it right or you don't. We want to hear those two magical words spoken to everyone around us who doesn't measure up: "You're fired!" (That is, of course, as long as *we're* still in the running to hear those elusive words, "You're *hired*!").

In that respect, John the Baptizer doesn't disappoint. Like the great prophets before him, he's keen on grabbing people's attention and then letting them *have it.*

To borrow a political phrase from years gone by, with a slightly more biblical twist, many of us love to read about John doing his thing, and we cheer him on: "Give 'em hell, John!" And that's *exactly* what John does.

Yes, it's in our human nature to love our prophets like we love our reality TV shows—*as long as we're in the audience watching.*

But when Simon starts picking on *me*; when Trump starts ripping into *me*; when the prophet's eyes turn toward *me* (and they always do, sooner or later), then I soon find out that my best efforts aren't anywhere close to being enough; that my every imperfection is being brought out for me, and everyone else, to see.

And, more often than not, when the prophet's eyes turn toward me, I, too, am just as likely to hear that one devastating word I love to hear Simon say to others with his head shaking and his arms crossed: "*NO.*"

But Jesus isn't like that.

Jesus didn't play this particular game often—though when he *did* turn up the heat, when he *did* rip into people, it was always directed at the good religious folks. It was always aimed toward the ones who "spoke for God."

If redemption were a reality show, then Jesus would be standing toe to toe with the Donalds and the Simons, overriding their decisions, and particularly welcoming and affirming the ones who were most harshly criticized and kicked out.

Jesus doesn't come to give us hell; Jesus comes to seek and to save us just as we are, "warts and all."

John the Baptizer comes to us exactly as we are and is quick to point out what's wrong, even when we may be getting some things right.

But Jesus comes to us and is quick to point out what's right, even when we may be getting *everything else* wrong.

I like John the Baptizer. He reminds me a lot of John Lennon, whom I love. But I'm trying to learn that I'm not called to follow John the Baptizer. I am called to follow Jesus. The critical and cynical part of me has trouble with this.

What the world needs more than anything are not more Simon Cowells or Donald Trumps or even John the Baptizers (Lord knows we have way too many already), but more of Jesus—more mercy, more grace, more forgiveness, more humility, and more love.

Some churches like playing reality show games with people and faith. It's time to stop. Rather than trying to weed everyone out down to *our* chosen few, let's start welcoming everybody in.

It's what Jesus would do.

Don't Let the Vegetarian Buzzards Get You Down

A friend challenged me to write an article on vegetarian buzzards. So . . .

In a recent article, I focused on one major thing the three great monotheistic religions of the world have in common: Father Abraham. Want a modest proposal for peace? Let all the children of Abraham agree not to kill each other.

I do not mean to downplay the unique claims and distinct beliefs of each religion. After all, I am an ordained Christian minister who seeks to follow Jesus, whom I profess to be the ultimate revelation of God's love to the world.

Since that article was published, however, I have been reminded of the events of September 11, 2001. Have I forgotten what the "Muslim world" wants to do to us Christians?

9/11. Unimaginable violent acts of hatred brought forth by people acting in the name of heaven.

However, Muslims around the world quickly condemned the attacks, saying that true Islam does not teach hatred and violence.

I know Christians who live among Muslims in other parts of the world, and I hear their stories of fellowship. I am getting to know some Muslims here in Starkville, and I have worshiped God—the Maker of Heaven and Earth—with Muslim friends at a Baptist service on a Sunday morning (yes, you read that correctly: Muslims worshiping God at a Baptist church). Because of these personal experiences, it's easy for me to distinguish a radical religious minority fueled by fear, hatred, and self-righteousness from the majority of Muslims who profess the message of peace, the message of goodwill toward others, and the message of love and devotion to the God of Abraham, Moses, and David.

The Crusades. A reminder that by no means do Muslims have a monopoly on religious fundamentalists who spew hatred and cause unspeakable, unimaginable destruction in the name of heaven. Yet I haven't heard of any Christians lately praising the terrible violence done in God's name during the Crusades.

Were they carried out in hatred? Yes. Out of fear? Probably. Lust for power? No doubt.

But for the glory of God? In service to Christ, the Prince of Peace? No. Of course not.

The Crusades do not stand alone in history. People have continued to commit atrocities in the name of Christianity.

Slavery? Done in the name of heaven and perceived, with the supposed blessings of the Apostle Paul, to be perfectly in keeping with being disciples of Jesus.

Segregation? Done in the name of heaven and defended fiercely by Christians leaders, pastors, deacons, and laity.

Beatings, lynchings, and even church bombings? Done in heaven's name by folks who went to church the next day feeling fully justified.

Shooting doctors who perform abortions? Celebrating deaths because of the sexual orientation of the deceased? All done in the name of heaven, in the name of God, in the name of Jesus . . . .

I'm a big fan of Donald Miller's book, *Blue Like Jazz* (Nashville: T. Nelson, 2003). I especially love the story he shares of confessing to non-Christians; confessing to others the horrible things done in the name of Christianity over the centuries and asking forgiveness. Don't judge Jesus by the actions of Christians, Miller emphasizes.

I'll leave it to my Jewish friends (who wish Christians *shalom* in the name of the one true God, the God of Abraham) to speak to the atrocities some people commit in the name of God and in the name of Judaism.

And I'll leave it to my Muslim friends (who wish Christians peace in the name of the one true God, the God of Abraham) to speak to the atrocities some people commit in the name of God and in the name of Islam.

But as for my fellow Christians—we who profess to worship the one true God, the God of Abraham, revealed in Jesus Christ, whom we profess to be God's only Son—let's be wary of making easy caricatures of Judaism and Islam.

We, too, are guilty of ignoring the commandments of God, the teachings of our Holy Bible, and the words of the One we claim as Christ. We, too, are quick to bow to the gods of power, the gods of greed, the gods of hatred, and the gods of war.

Which brings me to the challenge to write about vegetarian buzzards.

Vegetarian buzzards. That is what we are.

We become vegetarian buzzards—an oxymoron that cannot by definition exist—when we claim to love God but hate others. (At least, that's my understanding of 1 John 4:29-21; what's yours?)

So, to my friends of other religions and faith traditions around the world, please do not judge Christianity based upon the actions of some "Christians." In other words, don't let the vegetarian buzzards get you down.

And for all of us who claim the banner of Christianity, may the forgiveness of our neighbors and God's wildly reckless grace pour out even on an oxymoron like us—vegetarian buzzards one and all.

Ain't from 'Round These Parts

Many years ago, my wife, Jency, met and dated a *foreigner*.

He came from a distant place of which she knew little. Though he could speak English, at times it seemed like a somewhat different language—strange and unfamiliar phrasings, strange and unfamiliar emphases, strange and unfamiliar words, not to mention a heavy accent. In fact, Jency still occasionally refers to that boyfriend as "the great-looking guy with a wonderful accent from some faraway, exotic land."

It took about two years—give or take a few months—for West Tennessee to break the young college-aged man of his accent and language peculiarities. Desperate to fit in with other young men in West Tennessee, and having been teased and picked on because of his differences, he worked hard to lose his accent and his strange and unfamiliar words and phrasings.

And three years after he moved to Tennessee, Jency married that foreigner—an immigrant to Tennessee from the exotic world of New Orleans, Louisiana; she mourns the fact that I felt forced to essentially lose my "wonderful accent" that romantically set me apart as being from "some faraway, exotic land."

Lately, I've been thinking a lot about Joseph. You know, *that* Joseph—the one in the Bible with the Woodstock-era Joe Cocker multi-colored coat and all the jealous brothers. I've been thinking about how his brothers sold him into slavery. How he rose to a position of prominence. How his family came to Egypt for help when famine struck. How even after his death, his family remained in Egypt and were fruitful and multiplied. Eugene Peterson's *The Message* says, "They were very prolific—a population explosion in their own right—

and the land was filled with them." (This story is found in the first chaper of Exodus.)

Then there arose a king in Egypt who "knew not Joseph," who was a bit worried about all those foreigners in Egypt growing in numbers, and he saw the Israelites as a threat—as competition for food, land, wealth. Maybe he even thought about an eventual war for conquest. The obvious solution, then? Round 'em up. Control their whereabouts and their work lives. But the harder this king pushed to control the Israelite population, the more kids they kept having. Then he started murdering all the boy babies, ordering them to be drowned in the Nile.

It a horrible thing to ponder the depths of human cruelty when acting out of fear and hatred and competition, especially when the ones being cruel have forgotten their past and their friendship and their cooperation with their now-victims.

Will Campbell tells a story of meeting a couple of "foreigners" from a faraway land who ended up in his neck of the woods in middle Tennessee. He says he and other neighbors gave the Hispanic men—only one of whom could speak a little English—odd jobs here and there; primarily they did construction work.

Will heard some folks say they were "illegal aliens." Will, though, being a Baptist preacher, says his understanding of Christianity tolerates "no notion of 'illegal somebody' or 'alien anybody,'" and thus he counted them as simply "friends."[1]

I can't help thinking about Will's story and the story of Joseph and how the Israelites ended up as slaves in Egypt when I hear so much of the discussion and rhetoric today about immigration, especially when fellow people of faith—who hold the Bible in such high regard—seem to echo the fears and hatred of the Egyptian king who "knew not Joseph."

Our faith neither recognizes nor tolerates manmade state boundaries, national boundaries, language boundaries, religious boundaries, racial or ethnic boundaries.

Our prejudices and our self-interests may desire to classify men, women, and children—all of whom are made in God's image; all of whom God loves enough to die for them—as "undesirable," as "illegal," or as "alien," but our faith in the God of Abraham, our faith in God the Father of our Lord Jesus Christ, does not recognize or tolerate any notion of "illegal somebody" or "alien anybody."

I don't know what the government's plan of action should be regarding the immigration issue, but I do know what the response of us as people of faith should be to our neighbors, and, as we celebrate our twenty-first wedding anniversary next month, I'm glad that Jency was open to dating—and marrying—a foreigner.

"When a foreigner lives with you in your land, don't take advantage of him. Treat the foreigner the same as a native. Love him like one of your own. Remember that you were once foreigners in Egypt. I am God, your God." (Leviticus 19:33-34, The Message)

There is no longer Jew or Greek, there is no longer slave or free, there is no longer male and female; for all of you are one in Christ Jesus. (Galatians 3:28, NRSV)

Note

1. Will Campbell, *Soul among Lions: Musings of a Bootleg Preacher* (Westminster John Knox Press, 1999) 23–24.

When All the Colors Come Out

(or Grace for Those Who Go Down in the Flood)

This past Sunday, my sermon centered on Noah, the flood, and the rainbow. And also those verses in 1 Peter about Jesus preaching to the souls in prison; souls from way back in Noah's time; souls who did not obey and died in the flood. Jesus *preached* to them. God's mercy extended out to them after all, or so the Scriptures hint.

And there's the rainbow—the promise never to flood the earth again. Mercy. Grace. It's not just a sign to Noah and his family, but God's sign of mercy, grace, and hope to all people everywhere and all creatures everywhere, "to every living thing on earth."

Such grace is greater than all my sins, for as deep and treacherous as God's judgment may be, there's a wideness and a depth to God's mercy that is far, far greater.

I brought with me into this Flood sermon the dark, treacherous waters of depression.

My friend, Richard, killed himself a couple of weeks ago. Richard is the fourth (or possibly fifth) person I have known who has committed suicide. He's the third (or possibly fourth) in the last five years (one person's death was ruled a tragic accident, but I have reasons to doubt).

For some reason, God draws me to certain types of people; for some reason, God draws certain types of people to me; or maybe it's just evidence of the old saying, "birds of a feather flock together."

I guess that's why one my favorite contemporary hymns is the U2 hymn "Beautiful Day." (If you want my advice, listen to as much U2 as you can. The world would be a better place.) Yeah, life stinks, Bono acknowledges, but, like a true prophet, he can find a ray of hope in the darkest moments and declare it *is* a beautiful day. Like a true prophet speaking a word from the Lord, he can see the rainbow and is desperate to point that rainbow out to us, too.

Because after the flood, *all the colors came out!*

Because no matter how bleak life may be, there's always a rainbow on the other side.

I guess that in the end of it all, God comes to us in love with open arms seeking to heal us, to restore us, to comfort us, to aid us, to renew us, to bring us back into the presence from which we've never really escaped anyway (or so says Psalm 139).

In frantically, desperately dog-paddling my way through this sermon, I decided that no matter how bad times may be, or how dark life can get, eventually we all find the rainbow waiting for us on the other side.

On the other side.

For those of us who can catch glimpses of the rainbow here and now and can share it with others, thanks be to God!

But even for those of us who don't make it into the ark, even for those of us who drown in the floodwaters of life, I find hope in our Scriptures when they declare that not even death itself can separate us from the love of God!

That even for those who are taken by the flood, even then, after the flood, all the colors come out!

Thanks be to God. Thanks be to God! *Thanks be to God!*

Why I'm a "Welcoming and Affirming" Baptist

I recently sat on a discussion panel at one of the Baptist institutions of higher learning in which I once studied. We panelists shared our thoughts as we explored this question: "Can someone be a Christian and be gay?" The following is a brief synopsis of why I answered with a resounding "yes!"

Let's recall a few basic facts about the earliest believers in Jesus, that community of believers in Jerusalem:

• They existed as a small group within Judaism. They were Jews who believed Jesus was the promised Messiah for the Jewish people, and they still worshiped in the synagogues and in the temple.

• They kept, or at least gave verbal allegiance to, the Law of Moses—things like not eating shrimp or anything from pigs, and, of course, all the males having a minor surgical alteration to mark them as God's people.

• They "knew" what God was like; they "knew" how to live in a "right relationship" with God; and they "knew" that God would not (meaning could not) act against what they practiced based on the authority of the Scriptures.

• Oh, and they were not fond of Gentiles (anyone who wasn't a Jew); their actions essentially said "to hell with the Gentiles."

Now, to be fair, if a Gentile wanted to become a believer in Jesus, that Gentile could convert to Judaism, learn all the God-ordained actions of what to eat, what not to eat, and, of course, the males would have to get that minor surgical alteration. Then and *only then* could a Gentile become a follower of Jesus, the Jewish Messiah, and be in a "right relationship" with God.

There's a story in the eleventh chapter of Acts about some rebels who had the chutzpah to go forth into foreign lands preaching the gospel of Jesus Christ to the *Gentiles!* Worse, these heretics let Gentiles respond to the good news without first converting to Judaism!

The believers back in Jerusalem had to take action; they had to defend the faith against such false practices. They sent Barnabas out to Antioch, a letter of correction in hand, to investigate the situation and set everyone straight.

When he got there, though, Barnabas recognized the movement of the Holy Spirit, the power of the gospel of Jesus Christ, and the working of God *outside of* and even *in contradiction to* so much of what the Jerusalem believers "knew" to be true. Barnabas stayed among those Gentile believers for a while, and it was in Antioch, among those who were undoubtedly "getting it all wrong" and not truly in "right relationship" with God, that followers of Jesus were first called "Christians."

Now let's review a few basic facts about Baptists in America:

• We are ethnically Gentiles and not orthodox Jews. Many of us eat shrimp and pork products as freely and liberally as we desire.
• We are certainly not overly concerned with which males have had that minor surgical alteration (which in America has nothing to do with being God's chosen ones).
• And we are the beneficiaries, then, of the early heretics who dared to recognize God's movement *outside of* and *even in contradiction to* what the Jerusalem believers "knew" to be true.

We Baptists are now in the position of the early believers in Jerusalem. We have become so enslaved to our own understandings that we "know" what God will not (meaning cannot) do. We have labeled an entire group of people "Gentiles," separating them from us, and our actions essentially say to them, "to hell with you."

We insist that homosexuals must first conform to what we say and do before they can grow in a relationship with Jesus. In other words, we need to correct their errant ways, and, well, set everyone straight.

Some of us, though, have witnessed the movement of the Holy Spirit among and the power of the gospel of Jesus Christ within our homosexual friends. Some of us have experienced the working of God outside of and even in contradiction to the teachings and doctrines of the Baptist tradition.

Like Barnabas, I choose to be open to God, whose love endures forever, whose mercy knows no barriers, and whose grace is far greater than my limited understanding, my feeble interpretations, and my most certain beliefs of how to live in a "right relationship" with God.

We Baptists are being confronted today with the reality that God moves in ways that we are convinced God is not supposed to move; that God is, truthfully, bigger than and free from everything we "know" to be right.

This is why I am a "welcoming and affirming" Baptist—embracing, worshiping with, and serving alongside my gay and lesbian brothers and sisters.

Part 3
Of Willie, Cowbells, and Other Magnolia Matters

musings and mutterings about life in Mississippi

My Head's in Mississippi

(Of Providence and Starkville)

I was born in and raised just outside New Orleans, and when my sons were little, my family and I lived in the heart of Memphis. I dearly love both of these great cities.

Though I may have been born in and lived most of my life so far outside the state, the fact is that Mississippi runs all through my veins. As the great Top once said (as in ZZ Top), "My head's in Mississippi." My heart is, too.

My mother and all her kin hail from the Delta (just outside Dundee, and when you're from "just outside Dundee" you know you're from *deep* in the country). My father and all his kin hail from the southwest woods (just outside Bogue Chitto, and when you're from "just outside Bogue Chitto" you know you're from *deep* in the woods).

When I was a kid and all my friends would go visit cousins, uncles, aunts, grandparents, and so on, most of the time they just went a few houses down the street, or they might have ridden thirty minutes or so along the river to a neighboring parish. When my sister, Becky, and I would visit cousins, uncles, aunts, grandparents, and so on, Mom and Dad would pack us up in the car and drive us back *home* . . . to Mississippi.

It was here in Mississippi—in the summer of 1984—that I first truly fell in love. During my eleventh grade year, I was certain I'd marry that Mississippi girl. But since she lived in Tunica and I lived a day's drive away in St. Charles Parish, Louisiana, the relationship ended within a year (though we remain good friends to this day).

Of course I did fall in love again—even far deeper—and married *another* Mississippi girl. Jackson, Tennessee, may be where my wife lived most of her life before she married me, but Jency was *born* in Biloxi.

Although my parents left Mississippi to attend Tulane University, when it was time for me to face the fact that sooner or later I'd have to graduate high school and leave my beloved marching, concert, and jazz bands, there was only one choice: to join the Famous Maroon Band and live on campus at *the* Mississippi State University.

I loved every moment of being in the bands at State, and I became close friends with people who, though we were only together for two short semesters, played a pivotal role in my life. But something just wasn't right.

I left after my freshman year and attended Union University in Jackson, Tennessee—a school with no marching band. I've never been able to comprehend why, in spite of all the friends I made via the band and the music fraternity, Phi Mu Alpha Sinfonia, and how much I loved everything about State, I was still lonely, isolated, and deeply depressed for most of my freshman year there. So my journey took me to other universities, other graduate schools, and other states.

In spite of the terrific places I've been and the transforming experiences I've had since leaving Starkville in spring 1987, I've always had a deep, unspeakable sorrow that I couldn't manage to stay at Mississippi State.

One of the odd and frustrating things about faith is that it doesn't always make sense. I don't believe in predestination or anything like that, but I do believe in the Providence of God; I do believe God's hand moves us and guides us in ways that we cannot see and in ways that we cannot understand.

I am still amazed that after more than twenty years of yearning to have lived longer in Starkville, and to have been a part of Mississippi State University longer, I now live in Starkville and teach at MSU. My sons—who have spent most of their lives elsewhere and noticed my cowbell serving as a shelf decoration from house to house—now have their own cowbells. Jency, who has listened to me speak so fondly of Starkville and old MSU friends for more than twenty years, now gets to experience it herself.

As I think about all the places I've lived, I can't help recalling words I often heard while living in New Orleans. An MSU grad named Julia said, "I just *love* Mississippi, don't you?"

And, for almost a year now, as I awake every morning in Starkville, Mississippi, surrounded by all things maroon and white, I am reminded of that famous quote from Dorothy in the land of Oz, "There's no place like home! There's no place like home!"

Football Players and Law Breakers

Dr. Kent Sills (everybody called him "Doc Sills") was the director of bands at Mississippi State when I was a student back in the mid-eighties. I played trombone in the Maroon Band. Doc used to say—especially during football season, and *especially* when we went to road games—that if any of us got arrested, he wouldn't claim us. Furthermore, whenever we got out of jail for whatever the reason, we could go ahead and turn in our band uniforms and then tell people that we "*used* to be in the Famous Maroon Band."

I'm glad Doc Sills, let alone the Starkville Police, never visited my freshman dorm room on the third floor of Sessums Hall. On my wall hung an official "Mardi Gras Route—No Parking" street sign. It was a birthday present sent to me from one of my best friends back home in Louisiana. By "official," I mean it mysteriously (and unbeknownst to me) left its post along a parade route and somehow ended up wrapped as a present and mailed to my MSU post office box.

Now that I am an ordained minister, and a Baptist minister at that, I of course cannot condone such hooligan behavior displayed by one of my high school friends. But think of the what-could-have-been news headlines: *Maroon Band Trombonist Blows It: Trades Band Dreams for Stolen Sign (Future with Maroon Band is certain: "I don't know Montgomery," says Sills)*.

I am the first to admit that big-time college sports (i.e., Southeastern Conference) is one of the most exciting things in the world. I am also the first to admit that when I want to win football games, I look to the guys playing in the SEC West; when I want to

find a good brain surgeon, I look to the women and men who graduated from Tulane.

That view changed recently when I had a starting player from the
football team in one of the classes I teach at MSU. Good student—
motivated and disciplined with perfect attendance!

But then a terrible thing happened: two *other* football players from
MSU (Why couldn't it have been Ole Miss? Why?) had run-ins with
the law. Immediately, the high court in my mind began passing judgment. Typical college football players! No discipline!

Then I recalled my own reckless days of college life when I was a
hooligan enough to accept stolen goods.

Me—an A/B student!

Me—from a good home!

Me—with a band scholarship!

Well, as far as the good home goes, Dad also had a shady past: as a
student at Tulane, he was arrested for disturbing the peace. He and
other students were driving around New Orleans honking their horns
and getting everybody fired up for the Tulane/Georgia Tech game.
Dad could've blown his chance at law school. I could've blown my
chance with the Maroon Band. Now everybody's watching to see what
becomes of two MSU Bulldog players.

All of a sudden, I'm giving the high court in my mind a rest. I
don't want to downplay the seriousness of any offenses, especially if
drunk driving was involved (drunk driving killed my cousin).

But I look around at adults I know—from lawyers and doctors to
social workers and ministers, and even to judges and police officers—
who can tell some wild stories about their own high school and college
days, sometimes involving alcohol and drugs (I'll leave the stories to
them). I think back to my own criminal days for which I got away
with accepting a gift from a friend that, legally, he shouldn't have had
in the first place. I think back to my own father's noisy criminal past
(my dad, a good, decent, upstanding citizen and church deacon who
could easily compete with Mayberry's Sheriff Andy Taylor for the
Lifetime Integrity Award).

I wonder how any college students, especially those with the kind
of pressures facing SEC athletes (on the national stage, with tons of

adults' super-sized salaries depending on their ability to run or catch or tackle or throw), and, again, while by no means condoning criminal behavior, all I can say is I'm not going to say anything anymore. Twenty-something years later, with a Mardi Gras sign on the wall next to me as I type, who am *I* to judge?

Besides, Ronny—if you're reading this—that sign was one of my best surprise birthday gifts ever! And to Coach Dan Mullen, to the assistant coaches, and to *everybody* on the football team—GO STATE! From now on, though, let's *all* agree (myself included) to leave the scandalous behavior to Ole Miss students.

Willie, State, and an Ole Miss Conspiracy

Written in August 2009 after two Willie Nelson concerts had been announced—then canceled—in central Mississippi. By the time this book was going to publication, a third concert was set in north Mississippi and, yes, it was canceled. Willie—please come to Mississippi State!

One of the best concerts I've ever been to was on April 22, 1992, at the amphitheater on Mississippi State's campus. It was the Allman Brothers Band with Blues Traveler, and it was incredible. I even have "bootleg" cassettes of that show (if anybody has upgraded this show to digital, I'd be glad to provide a couple of blank CDs).

Because I've lived in other states for most of the last decade, that's also the last concert I've been to in Starkville. Now that I'm back in town, I'd like to see more concerts at the amphitheater.

May I suggest the next one?

Willie Nelson.

Yep, good ol' Willie. Twice in the past six months, he has announced concerts in our great state, and twice they've been canceled. The first one was at a casino around Philadelphia; the second was to be at the Veterans Memorial Stadium in Jackson. About the time I start making my plans to attend, the concerts get canceled.

A smart woman I know is convinced that Ole Miss is the source of everything that is wrong with the world. She won't even go to Oxford to pull for the Bulldogs when we play the Rebels because she says the "darkness" there is too strong; instead, she cheers for the Dogs from

Starkville as they, like Don Quixote, "march into hell for a heavenly cause."

I think this friend's arguments are beginning to get the better of me. For example, I have no hard evidence to prove this (actually I have no evidence of any kind), but I can't shake the hunch that Ole Miss is somehow behind the cancellation of Willie Nelson concerts in Mississippi.

It's a fierce accusation, I know, and I am ready to apologize to my Ole Miss neighbors if I'm proven wrong. The basis of my suspicion rests in a topic that we'd rather not talk about, but since, as Willie himself has sung, "there's always somebody who says what the others just whisper" ("Cowboys are Secretly Fond of Each Other," single, 2006), I'm going to point out the obvious: Ole Miss has a monopoly on federal-government-approved pot farming, and again—just being honest—a Willie Nelson concert in Mississippi may somehow be construed as, well, "unwanted competition."

There. We're all thinking it, and now we've all acknowledged it, so let's move on.

Leaving the Ole Miss conspiracy out of it, a Willie Nelson concert at Mississippi State makes perfect sense for several reasons:

• Willie loves farmers, and MSU is an agricultural school. Maybe Willie might even talk to a class or two about farming matters (he knows quite a bit about farm issues).

• Willie unites people. From beer-drinking rednecks to the aforementioned Ole Miss-crop-loving hippies; from politicos like Mike Huckabee to Jesse Jackson (both Baptist preachers, by the way, who like to be seen with Willie); from conservatives to liberals; from anarchists to socialists; from atheists to Pentecostals; from Jews to Catholics; from Hindus to Buddhists; from poor folks to rich socialites; from hard-core rockers to blues lovers; and from jazz devotees to fans of the golden days of the Grand Ole Opry—Willie brings everybody together, and he brings out the best in everybody.

• Who else but Willie can honky-tonk at the amphitheater on a Saturday night, and then lead us in grand ol' hymns and rafter-shakin' spirituals on a Sunday morning? (Willie, my Sunday morning pulpit is yours if you should feel so led).

I don't know who on State's campus is in charge of booking concerts, but dear Madam or Sir, please sign Willie . . . and soon! I'd go to the Humphrey Coliseum or Dudy-Noble Field if you want to make it that big, but nothing, and I mean nothing, will beat the intimacy of an evening outdoors at the amphitheater.

As a personal note to Willie: regardless of whether or not Ole Miss is to blame for the cancellations of your last two Mississippi performances, rest assured that you can trust your friends at MSU. I'll bet the university will even present you with a genuine MSU cowbell for you to ring at your next Farm Aid concert.

And to you, dear readers, lest any of you be concerned about this pastor writing about Willie, I guarantee you that I won't be the only minister present singing along with everything from "Good-Hearted Woman" to "Uncloudy Day." I've said it before, and I'll say it again, "Thanks be to God for Willie Nelson!"

Get Your Cowbells Ready, 'Cause Here Come the Tigers!

MSU vs. LSU, September 26, 2009. Depending on who you ask, LSU won the game 30-26. Most MSU fans, and even a few kind LSU fans, say otherwise. This was written a few days prior to the game.

"I *hate* LSU!" These may be some of the first words I ever heard. Today, if you ever meet my parents (especially my mother), you'll hear these words yourself.

Dad traces his disdain for the Tigers back to 1958. Actually, he never was a fan before then either, but his dislike for LSU "was really cemented" (his exact words) at the Tulane/LSU football game that year. Dad, a Tulane student at the time, recalls, "LSU was number one in the nation; Tulane was really bad, even for Tulane. LSU was trying to impress the national press, but only led 6-0 at halftime. The Green Wave ran out of steam, of course, and with a couple of minutes left in the game, the Tigers led 56-0. Coach Paul Dietzel sent his All-American runner, Billy Cannon, back into the game to score again. That was the first of *three* 62-0 routs by LSU [over Tulane]."

"I *hate* LSU!" With almost the same slow emphasis on the word "hate" that I had heard a zillion times from my parents, my friend Nolan shared his thoughts about the Tigers as he sat next to me at a Mississippi State/LSU baseball game this past spring.

Nolan tells of being in the Ole Miss band and traveling down to Baton Rouge ("a lot of Ole Miss folks hate LSU more than they hate Mississippi State," he said). The fans in Tiger Stadium were so intimidating that when the game was over and the band was leaving, they left in a special formation—all the guys formed a block around all the girls, and horn players held mouthpieces in their hands in case they needed to throw a punch for protection. According to Nolan, the band members made it to their buses and back up to Oxford unharmed; however, one of the tubas suffered an imprint of a brick in its bell.

"I *hate* LSU!" With almost the same slow emphasis on the word "hate" that I heard from my parents and from my friend Nolan, members of the Famous Maroon Band expressed their feelings as we were preparing to load the band buses and drive down to Jackson to play LSU. I was a freshman in the Maroon Band in 1986, and back then LSU wouldn't come all the way up to Starkville to play State (or perhaps Starkville refused to host LSU—I'm not sure which). A fellow band member even confessed that he hated LSU more than he hated Ole Miss.

A small group of drunken college-aged guys dressed in purple and gold decided it would be fun to sit near the MSU band. They sat right behind a couple of young families with children who sat next to us; they began cursing, yelling, and taunting us in the band, and taunting the families next to us. One of the mothers spoke firmly but politely, pointing out that there were plenty of available seats around the whole stadium, especially where huge clumps of LSU fans were sitting together. The drunk guys became more rude and more aggressive. The mother's protective instincts kicked in and she smacked the lead drunkard with her cowbell. Security came and escorted the drunken young men away; nothing was said to the mother—the whole band would have testified that she acted in self-defense.

"I *hate* LSU!" I'm already hearing that familiar phrase, with the same slow emphasis on the word "hate," as MSU and Starkville prepare to host the LSU Tigers this coming weekend. Whatever reasons forced the Dogs to play the Tigers down in Jackson during the 1980s, they are no longer relevant. In just a few days, Starkville will be swamped with people wearing purple and gold.

Being from Louisiana myself, most of my Louisiana friends were (and still are) LSU fans. Some attended LSU. And to my parent's dismay (especially my mother's), I no longer *hate* LSU; in fact, I really like them . . . but I love my Bulldogs more.

This Saturday, my 2-1 Dogs take on the 3-0 Tigers, and when MSU wins by a touchdown (if we do win, remember that I predicted it here first!), I'll be politely and lovingly hugging my purple-and-gold friends and trying to protect them from my maroon-and-white friends' cowbells.

That is, unless such prolonged direct exposure to the distinctly LSU attitude causes me to forget my Louisiana roots and my Christian-pacifist tendencies and with cowbell in hand I . . . on second thought, maybe I should leave my cowbell at home, just in case.

"The 'Neau" Will Always Be "The W" to Me

The Mississippi University for Women in Columbus may be getting a name change. In fall 2009, the name "Reneau University" was officially proposed. At the time of this book's publishing, it seems it may still be "The W" for some time to come.

My cousin Jenene is joining the faculty of the University of Illinois at Springfield. She tells people she graduated from "The W," which is and shall always be true. But when people try to look up "The W" from now on, they'll have a hard time finding it. "The W" (sometimes referred to as the Mississippi University for Women) is in the process of having its name changed to Reneau University.

Drastic name changes are not uncommon. We all know that it's Istanbul, not Constantinople; that it's John Mellencamp, not John Cougar; and that it's back to Prince, not The-Artist-Formerly-Known-as-Prince (unpronounceable symbol).

I will forever refer to Memphis State University as "Memphis State University"; I still cannot get used to the "University of Memphis" (for one, U of M reminds me too much of Ole Miss). I have several friends who graduated from Memphis State, not from "Memphis." Besides, for two days I was a member of the Memphis State Band, never the University of Memphis Band. My sons, however, don't remember Memphis State, and with great aggravation they continue to correct me: "It's the University of Memphis!" Sorry, folks, but it's "Memphis State."

My father still refers to Hattiesburg's institution of higher learning as "Mississippi Southern"; I've never known it as nor called it anything other than "Southern Miss." To which Dad replies, "Sorry, folks, but it's 'Mississippi Southern.'" On the other hand, I know of nobody who went to Mississippi A&M, and today we all proudly proclaim our love for and devotion to Mississippi State University ("Hail, dear ol' State!").

For the most part, it seems almost everyone has weathered such name changes fairly well.

There are notable exceptions, though. Take, for example, the incredible 1969 debut by the rock group Chicago Transit Authority, which, due to the unhappiness of the actual transit powers-that-be in Chicago, had to change their name to just "Chicago," and thus began a slow, two-decade decline into painfully mediocre pop music.

But that was nothing compared to what happened when the rock group Jefferson Airplane changed its name. In short, the revolutionary Jefferson Airplane eventually became the very good Jefferson Starship, which degenerated into simply Starship. People can enjoy "We Built this City" all they want, and had it come from just a one-hit wonder pop-radio group, it wouldn't seem so awful; but coming from the direct lineage of the Airplane . . . well, it's enough to make me thankful for the mediocre 1980s Chicago.

In both literature and film, there are several examples where drastic name changes correlate with drastically unpleasant changes in character: Dr. Jekyll becomes Mr. Hyde; Sméagol becomes Gollum; Benjamin Barker becomes Sweeney Todd; and Norman Bates becomes his mother, Mrs. Bates (well, sort of).

Scriptures, too, are fond of giving people new names, usually to good results: Abram becomes Abraham, Jacob becomes Israel, and Saul becomes Paul.

Sometimes name changes are tricky and can be disastrous, but sometimes they can be positive. Lest we forget, Angelo Giuseppe Roncalli became the renowned Pope John XXIII, who gave the world the great Second Vatican Council and opened "the windows of the Church to let in some fresh air."

Which brings me back to the Mississippi University for Women. I think "The W" will survive, and maybe it will even thrive. Cousin Jenene will certainly have trouble referring to her alma mater as something other than "The W," and people my age and older will never really make the adjustment—the potentially soon-to-be-named Reneau University will always remain "The W," much like Memphis State will always be, well, "Memphis State."

For this present generation, perhaps a transitional "The University Formerly Known as the Mississippi University for Women" will be helpful. And of course, the next generation, not being used to referring to the Mississippi University for Women as "The W," will likely have no problem fondly referring to Reneau University as "The 'Neau."

For the sake of all present and future students, I sure hope so.

As for me, I'm going to thank God for how much "The W" means to my cousin and my family, and then turn up the volume on Jefferson Airplane's "Somebody to Love."

The Truth about Favre and Pickin' Flowers

Written in fall 2009. We all know how Favre's decision worked out, and pull for Favre I did, until the NFC Championship, of course. Unfortunately, 2010 passed without a Flower-Pickin' Festival.

I'd like to address two rumors I've heard this week: first, that quarterback Brett Favre is retired; and second, that the upcoming 3rd Annual Pardon Johnny Cash Flower Pickin' Festival in Starkville is dead.

As to the first one, I paraphrase Mark Twain: rumors of Brett Favre's retirement have been greatly exaggerated.

I like Brett Favre. He's a good Mississippi boy, a *tough* Mississippi boy. A lot of people are mad at Brett, but I'm not. The Packers let it be known that they were through with their legendary quarterback. Mr. Favre knew in his heart (and bones and legs and arms) that he still had a little game left in him. In fact, in some ways Mr. Favre reminds me of another favorite tough Mississippi boy, Archie Manning.

I was just a toddler when Archie was rambling around Ole Miss, but from the time I was about three or four, I clearly remember Archie Manning as the face of my hometown team, the New Orleans Saints. When I was reaching my teenage years, the Saints decided Archie had nothing left to offer them (actually, new coach Bum Phillips let Archie go so he could bring in Kenny Stabler—a slightly older player who was moving on to his third team). I watched sadly as Archie played one year for the Houston Oilers before moving up to play one more year for the Minnesota Vikings. Neither was a good year for Archie or for either of those teams. But the tough ol' Mississippi boy still had some game in him, that's for sure.

I do remember Brett Favre—a different personality from Mr. Manning, yes—leading his Southern Miss Golden Eagles to huge upsets, and then I quickly became a Green Bay Packers fan. Another tough Mississippi boy makes good story. And, unlike the Saints with Archie, the Packers were able to put people around Brett who enabled him to work his magic.

Then many years passed, and the Packers decided their legendary quarterback had nothing left to offer them. Like Archie going to the Oilers, Favre led the New York Jets for one year and is now joining Archie in the ranks of tough ol' Mississippi quarterbacks having to play for Minnesota.

Okay. Yes. I, too, grew weary of the "is he or isn't he retired?" scenario over the past several months. But I, for one, still think Brett's got a good bit of game left in him.

Of course, nobody thinks of the Oilers or the Vikings when they think of Archie. It's Ole Miss and the New Orleans Saints. And in ten or fifteen years, nobody is really going to think of the Jets or the Vikings when they think of Favre (well, unless the Vikings get into the playoffs); they'll think of Southern Miss and the Green Bay Packers.

But until then, for this next football season at least, Favre is not retired; he is a Viking. And I'm rooting for the boy from Mississippi.

Now for the second rumor. A friend looked at me earlier this week and said, "The Pardon Johnny Cash Flower Pickin' Festival is not happening this year. It's officially dead."

I was the "chaplain" (for lack of a better term) at last year's festival, and I consider the founder, Robbie Ward, a friend. So I sent Robbie a message. "Robbie," I said, "I heard this week that it is 100 percent for sure the Festival is not going to happen; it's dead."

Robbie's immediate response was, "Remember what they said about Mark Twain's death. . . . Twain's response seems appropriate here, too."

I like Robbie. He's a good Mississippi boy, a *tough* Mississippi boy, though not tough in the same manner as Archie Manning or Brett Favre. And he's from the Delta, which makes him as good as kinfolk to me. As I hear tell, he and the festival have been "counted out" each of the previous two years, and each of the previous two years the festival has occurred, continuing to draw interest and devotion from Cash fans around the world.

Since I happen to love everything about the Flower Pickin' Festival, I'm ecstatic to hear that the rumors of its death have been greatly exaggerated.

So pay no attention to those rumors. During the weekend of October 16–18, you'll find me right here in Starkville, enjoying the Flower Pickin' Festival and all things Johnny Cash. The rest of the fall, you can find me in front of my television, cheering for Brett Favre and hoping his year with the Vikings turns out better than Archie's.

Now then, what about the rumor I heard that Willie Nelson is coming to Mississippi State?

Prayer and the Need for Jumbotron Entertainment

Written on Saturday, October 3, 2009, prior to the MSU/Georgia Tech football game.

"Nice to see the faculty raises being put to good use!" joked a school administrator to a Mississippi State University professor, referring to the huge banner of football coach Dan Mullen hanging along the side of one of the stadium ramps.

Laughing, the professor responded, "Hey, we have no delusions about what's most important around here!" Then the conversation turned back to the football game they were heading to attend.

Huge maroon banners hang all around the outside of the stadium (such as the one with Coach Mullen pictured on it). The banners announce that something electrifying is in the air.

Anybody, however, who has been *in* the stadium has been "wowed" by the super-gigantic high-definition video boards ("high-definition video boards" as used here means "the big ol' jumbotron"). No one can deny that so far this season, an exhilarating energy surrounds the Bulldogs, the stadium, the campus, and even Starkville.

With its crystal-clear replays (my students this week *swore* that with the jumbotron, it was undeniable that State pushed the ball across the goal line against LSU), and the surging music to keep the crowd pumped up, the MSU jumbotron is now the envy of our Southeastern Conference neighbors (Google "MSU jumbotron" sometime).

But, as the conversation between the professor and his friend illustrate, this jubilant energy doesn't exist in a vacuum. In stark contrast to the new decorations and equipment at Mississippi State's football stadium, the state of Mississippi is struggling economically, and the state's universities are looking at serious budget cuts.

"A six-million-dollar television set," says another Starkville resident. "If I wanted to watch the game on TV, I'd just stay home and watch it on TV. Imagine what that money could have provided for the *educational* purposes of the university. Imagine what that money could have provided for the people of Starkville. Six million dollars for a TV set, and I'm out here working my butt off on a Habitat [for Humanity] house." (Note: This resident and lifelong Bulldog fan sat in his stadium seat for the entire game against LSU last week.)

As far as I know, the jumbotron and the banners were paid for with private booster funds, rendering the "faculty raises" exchange moot, yet the latter resident's comments about funding the university's educational purposes, and even funding needs for the community, remain valid.

When academic departments are scrambling to offer enough classes for the students—yet weighing that against the number of instructors they can afford—it does shine a light on our priorities.

When Habitat houses are being funded and built by volunteers with what little money and time they have to give, it does indeed shine a bright light on our priorities as people in a community.

All that said, with my ministerial connections and sympathies for Habitat for Humanity, I'm at home getting ready to attend tonight's MSU/Georgia Tech game instead of being out with my friend working on a house this morning.

All that said, with my teaching connections to the university, I'm climbing the banner-decorated ramps to the upper level of Davis-Wade stadium with my family for tonight's game.

All that said, I assure you I will get pumped up by the surging music and thoroughly enjoy the clear, larger-than-life replays on the jumbotron.

College sports is big money and big business. While I don't adhere to the "if you can't beat them, join them" philosophy, I do try to take to heart Reinhold Niebuhr's prayer, which has been adapted somewhat and become known as the Serenity Prayer:

> God, give us grace to accept with serenity
> the things that cannot be changed,
> Courage to change the things which should be changed,
> and the wisdom to distinguish the one from the other.
>
> Living one day at a time, enjoying one moment at a time,
> Accepting hardship as a pathway to peace,
> Taking, as Jesus did, this sinful world as it is, not as I would have it
> . . . .

The jumbotron and the banners are here. That's the way it is. I pray I do what I can to help with the real problems that bother me, such as budget cuts and poverty issues. And in the meantime, I'll join faculty and ministers and Habitat workers tonight with all the fans as we fill Davis-Wade stadium and feel good about our football team. Go State!

The Double-Wide Gospel according to Karen

Roger Miller sings about trailers, be they for sale or rent. Kid Rock reminds us that unlike Ice Cube, he ain't outta Compton but straight outta trailer. And Jimmy Buffet, the son of a son of a sailor, is just glad he doesn't live in a trailer.

There certainly is a negative connotation given to trailers and the folks who live in them. Some of my favorite childhood memories, however, are of visiting cousins in rural Mississippi: the sounds of Skynyrd emerging from Jeff's open window in his trailer bedroom, and Jennifer, Jenene, and my sister and I jumping on the trampoline out back.

Years later, as a married man with kids and living in a midtown Memphis duplex, I preached many weekends at a rural church in Clay County, Mississippi. We'd drive down on Saturday afternoons and enjoy the space and freedom offered by the church's parsonage: a double-wide parked next to the church. Wide-open rooms inside (a big difference from a crowded duplex) and wide-open spaces outside.

There's a nostalgic side of me that, despite the stereotypes and the condescending social attitudes, has always longed to clear some land in the Mississippi woods and set up house in a trailer.

Karen Spears Zacharias isn't from rural Mississippi, but she is from the Georgia countryside, grew up along the Chattahoochee River, was bitten by the deadly (well, not in her case) water moccasin, and, according to her website bio, "had her first kiss in a trailer, smoked her first and last cigarette in a trailer, asked Jesus into her heart on bended knee in a trailer, fell madly in love in a trailer . . . and gave birth to her firstborn child in a trailer."

Oh, and her brand-spankin' new book is called *Will Jesus Buy Me a Double-Wide? ('Cause I Need More Room for my Plasma TV)* (Grand Rapids: Zondervan, 2010).

Karen, once a newspaper journalist, turns her reporting skills loose against evangelists who collect offerings to feed their own lavish lifestyles, and also against those who preach a God of health, wealth, and big happy smiles. But what could have been an easy (and necessary) denunciation of TV evangelists and purveyors of the so-called "prosperity gospel" is instead a collection of real stories of real people living real lives in the real world where God *also* lives. The bulk of the book focuses on lives of faith from people living in the streets to folks living in suburbs to families living in—you guessed it—trailers.

Karen's stories will make you howl with laughter, cry in empathy, and occasionally seethe in righteous indignation. Through it all, the truth of God's loving presence and grace is revealed not in feel-good, get-nice-stuff promises, but in the pain, loss, love, and hope of all God's children.

While so much of our "Christian" culture reflects our materialist American culture, Karen's book will certainly appear out of place on many Christian bookstore shelves, but that's exactly where it needs to be. Karen proudly places herself and her faith not in stained-glass cathedrals and successful executive suites, but on the streets and in the trailer parks.

Karen's book and her theology have earned their place on my bookshelf right alongside my Will Campbell collection. (Will Campbell is another prophetic voice who walked away from the ministerial big leagues and high salaries to live among the rural poor and oft-demeaned "white trash" from which he came.)

While some may pray for God to give them a mansion and a Mercedes-Benz, Karen just says she may retire one day with her husband and live in God's blessed presence in an Alabama double-wide. Something tells me that when I visit, I might hear the sounds of Skynyrd coming through their screen door.

Of Egg Bowls,
the Maroon Band,
and Things that
Never Change

November 28, 2009.

Things sure have changed since I was in the Famous Maroon Band. Back in 1986, I was a trombonist (one of among thirty-plus trombone players). Dr. Kent Sills was director of bands; Mr. Bob Taylor ("Mr. T") was assistant director. MSU football legend Rockey Felker was in his first season as the Bulldogs' head coach.

At the end of our summer band camp in August of that year, Coach Felker came over to give us a pep talk. The loudest guy in the band stood up and yelled, "Hey, Coach! How badly are we going to beat Ole Miss this year?" (For the record, and to show respect to my Aunt Helen over in Senatobia, whom I love even though she roots for the wrong school, we lost that year.)

Back then, the Maroon Band sat next to the student section. Doc Sills would keep one eye on the game at all times, one eye on the game clock, and one eye on more than 300 overly excited college students for whom he was responsible (yes, I'm convinced Doc had three, or maybe even four, eyes).

Doc waved his hands frantically at us, and somehow we knew what song we were to play; and we were *always* about to play something. Sometimes Mr. T would take over. He simply scribbled a word or two on a small dry-erase board, held it up high, and immediately we were playing.

This weekend, for the first time in twenty-three years, I had the opportunity to sit with the MSU Famous Maroon Band during the Egg Bowl. And yep, things sure have changed since I was in the band.

Doc has gone on to that great band hall in the sky and is waiting to wave his hands frantically at us all again one day. Mr. T is now *Doctor* Taylor and hasn't been at MSU in who knows how long. I hear he's about to retire.

Ms. Elva Kaye Lance is now the director of bands (herself a Doc Sills Maroon Band alumna). Drs. Clifton Taylor and Craig Aarhus are the associate and assistant directors.

These days everyone has big televisions in their college stadiums, and like TVs at home, they come with commercials and other entertaining tidbits between close-ups and instant replays of what's happening on the field. MSU's Scott Field at Davis-Wade Stadium is no different.

Today's directors have headsets and microphones. In addition to the action on the field, the sidelines, and the actions of more than 300 overly excited college students carrying expensive musical equipment, Ms. Lance and Drs. Clifton and Aarhus converse directly with marketing folks up in the press box to manage "air" time. Marketing folks need to know when the band will play so they don't run competing commercials over the band, and so the band doesn't play over the commercials. It was a tricky during the first couple of home games with the new jumbotron, but the kinks appear to have been worked out, and they are all working together to maximize the entire stadium experience for everyone.

Today's Maroon Band follows color-coded pre-printed plastic-covered song-title cards instead of frantically waving hands or scribbled words on dry-erase boards. They sit in the end zone rather than with the students (which actually gives both groups of students more room to move).

As I sat with the Maroon Band and cheered on the Bulldogs, I realized that though things have indeed changed, much has also remained the same.

Doc's gone and Mr. T has left, sure. But Doc's former student is now head director, and Mr. T's son is a student manager of the Maroon Band.

Coach Felker is no longer the head coach; Dan Mullen, with his national championship ring, is. But Rockey Felker is still part of the Bulldogs' staff and is a well-respected figure on campus and in the community.

At the end of the game, I walked into the low brass section and spoke to two trombonists and a baritone player. Riley, Charles, and Armed spoke of old high school classmates who went to that *other* school, old high school band members who now play for the *other* band. They spoke of how it's been a tough but exciting year to be a Bulldog. And they reminded me that even as band members, they understand there are two seasons of football every year: the first season consists of eleven games, and the second season is the Egg Bowl.

I wonder if Coach Mullen made his way over to the band at the end of band camp just before school started like Coach Felker did in 1986. If he did, I'm certain the loudest student must've asked, "Hey, Coach! How badly are we going to beat Ole Miss this year?" (For the record, and with love for my Aunt Helen, whom I called from the end zone to offer ministerial counseling, we *killed* 'em this year!)

Win or lose. Low-tech or high-tech stadiums. 1986 or 2009. The rivalry between MSU and "that school up north" will *never* change.

www.ingramcontent.com/pod-product-compliance
Lightning Source LLC
Chambersburg PA
CBHW062059270326
41931CB00013B/3143